Real Estate Investing – Flipping Houses

Complete Beginner's Guide on How to Buy, Rehab, and Resell Residential Properties the Right Way for Profit. Achieve Financial Freedom with This Proven Method

James Connor

professional before attempting any techniques outlined in this book.

By reading this document, the reader agrees that under no circumstances is the author responsible for any losses, direct or indirect, which are incurred as a result of the use of information contained within this document, including, but not limited to, — errors, omissions, or inaccuracies.

Table of Contents

Introduction *1*

Chapter 1: Basic Concepts *3*

House Flipping: What is it? 3

Wholesale Flipping 3

Rehabbing 4

How Does House Flipping Work? 5

How Much Can You Make Flipping? 7

Taxes You Need to Pay as A Home Flipper 8

Ordinary Income Tax Implications When Flipping Properties 9

When is Capital Gains Tax Applicable to House Flipping? 10

Does Flipping Still Work in Today's Market? 10

Chapter 2: The Renovating/Rehab Process *15*

Appraise the Investment Property 15

Make a Checklist 16

Create a Budget 16

Locate The Appropriate Contractor 17

Get the Needed Permits 18

Rehabbing the Property 19

Begin the Cleanup Phase 19

Begin with Enhancements to The Interior 19

Enhance the Exterior..20

Finalizing Stage 21

Chapter 3: Get Your Financing in Place22

Getting Financing 22

Things to Put in Place Before You Apply for A House Flipping Loan.............................23

Develop a Business Plan for Every Flip......................24
Get Accurate Estimates of All Costs of Renovation . 25
Develop Your Network 26

Ways to Get Financing 26

Bank Financing...26
Personal Loans..27
Line of Credit 28
Hard Money Loan...29
Loan from Family and Friends 30
Look for a Financing Partner 31
Real Estate Crowdfunding Sites................................32
401(k) Financing...32

Your Financial Inventory.........................33

Credit Score/Credit History 34
Your Earnings 34
Your Resources 35
Debt...36
Familiarity with Investing...37

Chapter 4: Locate Your Agent(s) 38

Is Your Housing Market Suitable for Flipping
Houses? 39
An Agent Can Locate the Appropriate House for You
....39

An Agent Offers You Market-Driving Tips When Remodeling...41

An Agent Offers You Advise On When-to-Sell 42

What Kind of Agent Should You Choose? 43
Dual Agents 44

How to Choose a House Flipping Agent 46
Experience 46

Has Time for You 47

Devoted to their Job.. 48

Inspired by Relationships 48

Capable of Learning 49

How to Get Your Real Estate License 49

What Can You Use a Real Estate License for? 51

Is it Compulsory to get a Real Estate License to Flip Homes? 51

Benefits of Having Your Real Estate License as A Rehabber 51

Chapter 5: Where You Should Buy? 55

How to Choose the Right Real Estate Farm Area 55
Choose a Farm Area Close to Home...........................55

Investigate Your Farm Area..58

Pick a Farm Area with Clear Boundaries 60

Ensure Your Farming Area Is the Appropriate Size. 61

Check your Farm Area's Numbers 61

Piecing It All Together 63

How to Develop Authority in Your Farm Area for Real Estate **64**

Direct Mail 64
Knocking on Doors 65
Door Hangers 65
Facebook Advertising 66
Take Part in Online Local Forums 66
Meetup Groups and Local Events 67
Get Your Website Ranked on Google Using Local Search Terms 67

Chapter 6: Who Should You Buy From? *69*

Buying from Owners with Equity **69**

Buying from Absentee Owners with Equity **70**

Buying from Owners Without Equity **71**

Buying Foreclosures at Auction **71**

Buying (REO) Bank-Owned Foreclosures 72

Choosing the Best Option for You **72**

Chapter 7: How to Locate the Best Deals *75*

Use the MLS 75
Become a Part of a Real Estate Investment Group .. 76
Search for Auctions 77
Talk to Wholesalers 78
Use Classifieds 78
Find an Agent 79
Use a Short Sale 80

Use REO..81
Seller Direct 81
Take a Drive Around 82
Check The Internet for Listings.............................82

Chapter 8: What is the Financial Formula for Flipping Homes? *84*

ARV or After Repair Value Formula........ 84

70% Rule Formula 84

Maximum Buying Price........................... 85

Expected Return on Investment.............. 85

The Formula for Offer Price.................... 86

Chapter 9: How to Make Offers............ 87

Crafting a Good Offer...............................87
Run a Comparative Market Analysis (CMA) 87
Consider Market Indicators.. 88
Determine The Motivation of the Seller 89
Learn About Other Offers on the Home 90
Get a Pre-Approval Letter if it Is a Financed Deal .. 90
Make A Larger Down Payment.................................... 91
Get an Attorney to Analyze the Offer 91

Engaging in Negotiations 92

Best Bidding Strategies 92

Open negotiations................................... 92
Start your bid low..92
Stay Calm 93
Play Hard to Get..93
Reach Out to Sellers Directly 93

Sealed Bids 93

Holding Deposits 94

Seller Counteroffers and Responses 95

Agreeing to The Terms 96

Rejecting/Refusing The Terms 96

Make a Counteroffer... 96

Chapter 10: Doing Your Due Diligence 98

The Legal Due Diligence.......................... 98

Due Diligence Tasks................................. 98

Do Your Homework.. 99

Go Through the Title History 100

Take a Look at Homeowners Association Restrictions and Covenants...101

Inspect The Property 102

Preparing for The Inspection of a Property 102

What a Home Inspection May Not Entail104

General Home Inspection 105

(WDO) Wood-Destroying Organisms Inspection.. 106

Lead-Based Paint Inspection 107

Radon Gas Inspection 107

Run Your Numbers Once More..............108

Steps to Take if the Numbers Are Not Right 109

Request for a Reduction in Price 110

Walk Away from The Deal...110

Chapter 11: Hiring Contractors 112

What Type of Contractor Do You Need? **113**

Finding the Right Contractor for Your Project **114**

Places to Find Your Contractor **115**
Referrals from Real Estate Investment Clubs (REIC) 115
Ask Subcontractors 116
Check Out Your Farm Area 116
Check Hardware Stores 116
Check Online 116

Questions to Ask Before You Hire a Contractor **117**
Have You Worked for Someone Similar? 118
How Long Have You Been in This Job? 118
Do You Work Alone? 118
Is There Any Area You Don't Work On? 119
Are You Presently Working On Any Project? 119
Do You Have the Required License? 119
Do You Have Insurance? 120

Signs to Look Out for When Choosing a Contractor **121**
Get Numerous Bids 123
Analyze the Job 124

What to Do About an Unreliable Contractor **124**

Understand Your Options of Payment ... **125**

Draw Up a Written Contract **125**

After Hiring a Contractor **127**
Keep detailed records 128

Release Payments Wisely 128

Be Aware of the Limit for the Final Bill 129

Know When You Can Deny Payment 129

Take Advantage of a Sign-Off Checklist .. 129

Chapter 12: Managing Your Rehab 131

Make a detailed plan 132

Don't Assume 132

Prepare the Scope of Work 133

Make Sure You Are All in Agreement 134

Dealing with Service Providers 135

Do Not Alter Your Decisions 136

Have a Contingency in Place 137

Don't Pay Contractors for Work Before Completion

.... 137

Ensure You Are Physically Present 138

Know Your Suppliers 139

Hire an Expert 140

Chapter 13: Agent Versus FSBO 141

Is it Compulsory to Hire Real Estate Agents? 141

FSBO or For Sale by Owner: What Does it Mean? 141

Agent vs. FSBO: Fees 142

Marketing 143

Time 143

Negotiation 144

Legal Assistance 145

Which Is the Ideal Option For You? 145

Chapter 14: Staging 146

Staging A Home: What Does it Mean? 146

Does Staging Work? 147

Use Neutral Colors 147

Clean and Clean Some More 148

Keep Things Fresh 148

Let There Be Light 149

First Stage the Vital Rooms 150

Rent Some Furniture 150

Don't Ignore the Curb 151

Chapter 15: The Closing Process 153

What Is a Closing? 153

House Closing Process for Sellers 154

Negotiating 154

Closing Costs 155

Agent Percentage 156

Buyer's Due Diligence 156

Closing 157

When Is Your Property Categorized as Sold? 158

Conclusion 160

Bibliography .. Error! Bookmark not defined.

Introduction

At some point, you have probably heard people talk about real estate investment. For many people, it is an easy way to make money, especially when it comes to flipping houses. Maybe your interest was triggered by shows about flipping you saw on television, or you have a close friend who is earning a lot of cash from real estate. Now, you are interested in going into the business, but you don't know where to begin.

The fact is, lots of other people have been in the same place you are right now. Even worse, many of them were unable to attain success when they finally gave it a try, while some were able to hit the right buttons and become successful in real estate. So what was the difference? Why were a few of them successful, and others were flops? How can *you* be among those successful individuals?

Here's the thing: you are already on the right path. By buying this book, you have taken a significant first step. In this book, you will learn all you need to know about investing in real estate and rehabbing homes. You will also learn how to find the best home to flip and how to get the financing you need.

With this book, you will develop the knowledge you need to buy, rehab, and sell properties for profit. We will look into these topics and a host of others related to real estate investment. I do not promise that there won't be obstacles on the way. However, I am confident that when you are through with this book, you will have a comprehensive understanding of all you need to know to become a prosperous rehabber. Also, if you effectively use all the information offered by this book, you will be able to sell your first home and many more for continued profits.

Now, let's begin this journey to becoming a successful real estate investor.

Chapter 1: Basic Concepts

House Flipping: What is it?

House flipping is when an individual makes the choice of buying a property to fix it up and quickly resell it. The individual buys the property and raises the value by renovating it before selling it for profit within a few months.

There are two major kinds of real estate investment you will be coming across as an investor in real estate, which we will discuss below:

Wholesale Flipping

Wholesaling has to do with buying a property and reselling it to another investor immediately, for a profit. This mostly takes place the same day or at the same closing table. Here, you rarely have to do any form of repairs on the property before selling it to some other investor.

As a wholesaler, you are only reselling the same property you purchased, but for a profit. If you want to be successful as a wholesaler, you must be excellent at negotiating and should be able to persuade sellers to let go of properties at a price lower than the market value, while still convincing buyers to buy at higher than the market value. As a wholesaler, you sell homes for a profit in only a few days, which means you get faster paydays and the possibility to engage in more deals than those involved in other forms of investment.

Although wholesaling is fast, there are a few downsides to it. First, you need to have investors on hand who are willing to buy your property. When it comes to wholesaling, the absence of a ready buyer means no deal. Also, based on how you drew your contract and the amount you placed in escrow, you might need to pay back your seller if you have problems finding a buyer. It is ideal to have prospective buyers ready before you make the seller an offer. This way, you have a lower risk of losing cash. Sometimes, the money you lose might substantial, but the primary damage would be to your reputation. If the news reaches others that you have a negative impact on homeowners, others may not be interested in collaborating with you. If you feel wholesaling is not ideal for you, there is a more common type of real estate investment, known as rehabbing.

Rehabbing

Rehabbing is when an investor buys a property, renovates it and upgrades it before selling it for a higher price. These projects have a life span of four or more weeks, depending on the level of work that needs to be completed during the renovation. The process is also known as "fix and flip," and it is one of the most popular methods of investing in real estate today, and not without good reason. Rehab properties can provide investors with a considerable profit margin while also aiding them to expand their network and portfolio.

Property owners who renovate their homes to increase the value of the property or for personal use, also fall under the category of rehabbing. This is the case even if they have no plans to sell off the property.

There are a host of other methods to flip homes beyond rehabbing and wholesaling; however, these are the most popular. In comparison to wholesaling, there are a lot of more options open to a rehabber, that will provide a broader opportunity to get returns. With this in mind, the rest of this book will pay more attention to the rehab aspect of flipping homes.

How Does House Flipping Work?

To flip a property the right way involves a reasonable amount of work. You need to follow a few steps which will be discussed below:

- Find: Search for properties that will make fantastic deals. Here, you are on the lookout for people who have an interest in selling their homes. There is a range of reasons individuals want to sell their homes. For a few of them, selling the house can help them fix a pending challenge, while for others, the home may be a problem they want to get rid of. Your objective should be to find these people and help them solve their problems. However, you need to have a budget and be aware of the highest amount you can invest in buying a property.

• Search for Financing: Next, you will need to look for a way to finance your house flip. With this, you will be on the lookout for lenders who can provide you with funding based on the value of the property. If you have the capacity, you can invest your own funds.

• Renovate or Fix: The next step in the process is to renovate or repair the home. This is the step that separates those who are successful from those who fail. To properly do the job, you need to pay attention to contractors, monitor the cost of repair, and remain within your timeframe and budget to develop homes people will want to buy. You also need to have a knowledge of negotiation with contractors and how to pay them the right amount to ensure they will do the job right.

- Flip: If the process is followed correctly, you will have a completed property at a reasonable price. This is the period you advertise your home for sale and learn ways to sell to make sure you get a good profit on your investment.

How Much Can You Make Flipping?

You can earn a lot from flipping homes, especially if you invest these returns into flipping more properties. The more places you flip, the more your profits will keep rising. If you check out what flippers earn per flip, you will see that house flippers are not just talking, they are making a tremendous amount of cash.

In the United States, the aggregate profit margin for flipped homes is $29,342 ("The Average Gross Margin in a House Flip", 2018). Although this is a pretty decent profit, you will be able to make more profit if the properties you are flipping sell in the range of $100,000 or more. These properties come with a 54 percent ROI, which makes it the most lucrative price range for house flipping.

The amount of money you can make from flipping a property is also dependent on where you are located.

In 2013, flippers in Massachusetts made a gross profit of $103,384 on each home on an average, while flippers in California pulled in $99,999 for each property in 2013. New York, New Jersey, Maryland, and Washington are also states that have helped flippers make lots of profit ("6 Best States to Flip a House in USA – Oracle Fields", 2018). If you can flip a home in one of these states, then you will be able to make some serious cash on each flip.

Even though there are average earnings, you have the potential to make more of this or way less, depending on your skills. You need to understand the rate of success and failure before you head into this business. However, even though you stand to make a lot from flipping homes, you need to make accommodations for taxes, which may take a sizeable part of your earnings.

Taxes You Need to Pay as A Home Flipper

For many people, this might be the sad part of flipping. However, you will need to pay taxes on whatever profits you make. If you have been categorized as a dealer by the IRS, the revenue from your flipped property would be taxed using your ordinary income tax rate.

To calculate your profit, you need to subtract all your costs, which include the price of the purchase, from your final sales price. For active investors who earn active profits, the tax bracket falls within 10 to 37 percent (Ivy, 2019).

The IRS states that a dealer in real estate buys a property and sells it to clients in the typical course of their business or trade. Lots of rehabbers are categorized as dealers because they hold on to properties for a short time, and most of their earnings come from flipping properties. Even part-time house flippers may be classified as dealers and would be taxed using ordinary income rates.

In contrast, returns you make from properties you hold for over 12 months are privy to a more beneficial long-term capital gain range of around 0 – 20 percent. An investor can make the choice of occupying the property or renting it out (Ivy, 2019).

Ordinary Income Tax Implications When Flipping Properties

If you are categorized as a dealer, the returns from a flip will be taxed using your dominant ordinary income rate. The range of ordinary income tax rates falls between 10 and 37 percent. Also, the profit is liable to self-employment tax of around 15.3 percent, which is twice the amount you will pay as a W2 employee.

As a dealer, the tax implication on each flip could range from as high as 53.3% to as little as 25.3%, based on your tax bracket. What this means is, you have to bear in mind that all of your profits do not come to you, but rather, a vast part belongs to the IRS (Ivy, 2019).

When is Capital Gains Tax Applicable to House Flipping?

If you are lucky enough not to fall in the dealer category, and you get most of your revenue from purchasing and selling properties after a year, then your taxes will be at the lower capital gains rates on the returns you get from the sale.

If you are serious about going into the business of flipping houses, either as a part-timer or full-timer, then you need to reach out to a professional CPA or accountant who can aid you in structuring your business in a way that would ensure your taxes fall in the lowest bracket possible.

Does Flipping Still Work in Today's Market?

In the past, flipping houses was an ideal chance for an individual with extra funds and an excellent eye for renovation to make money. The market was filled with unoccupied homes from waves of foreclosures caused by the housing crash that blew up some years before. You could purchase a property from a bank, do the needed repairs, put on a coat of fresh paint, and list it for a higher price on the market.

However, with the real estate market heading back to the level it was before the recession, the amount of properties being listed on the market every month is not as high. A day after listing a property, bidding wars begin, which results in homes being sold way beyond the asking price in many circumstances. Buyers who are ready to reside in the homes they buy are finding it difficult to find cheap properties, which implies it is even more difficult for investors in search of homes at low prices.

With these factors in mind, the question many investors tend to ask is: "***Does flipping still work in today's market?**"*

The answer to this question is *yes*. Flipping is starting to become a recognized business, as an increasing number of organizations like Offerpad, Opendoor and Zillow are providing fast purchases of homes in cash with the aim of fixing and selling for returns. These organizations give more choices to property sellers, but their existence brings about a more competitive market for other investors.

Still, this does not prevent individuals from making

an effort to flip properties. However, the requirements for investors who want to attain success are starting to change. In addition to having the capacity to locate the appropriate house and a homeowner who has an interest in selling, you also need the financial ability to get past the stages of renovation and marketing before you can see your returns.

To enhance your possibilities of earning cash from flipping properties, here are a few more steps you can take:

- **Invest differently:** Instead of searching for homes on numerous listing services, try locating those that have not been listed on the market but whose owners are likely to have an interest in a sales offer. You can effectively do this by going through the data of the property and deciding which ones will make a worthwhile investment. Also, accessing property records (which you can get at the office of the local assessor) can offer you information on property taxes and how long the same individual has owned a property. You can also try to buy a property and hold on to it in order to get income from rent. However, all of the management and maintenance tasks associated with that property will fall squarely on you.

- **Begin small**: If you want to go into the business of flipping homes, don't start with a property with lots of plumbing issues and a flawed foundation. You have a better chance of turning in profit with a property that does not require *too* much work, but that can be sold off at an increased price with a few small repairs and competent staging. It will also be less challenging to lure lenders when there is not as much risk involved, particularly if you are going into real estate for the first time.

You won't make an enormous profit at first. However, you won't have bought a money drainer either. The instant you can make sure the house does not have any hidden issues via inspection and you have checked all the legal matters with regard to the property (which we will be discussing further in this book), you can now attract the right buyer by adding a few cosmetic changes.

- **Wait for a downslide in the economy**: This is not a positive strategy when it comes to investing in real estate, but in house flipping, you require a good number of homes listed on the market if you want a great deal on homes to flip. The only method of ensuring a surplus influx of homes is when people are unable to afford to reside in them anymore. And this implies an economic nosedive.

Admittedly, it is more difficult to sell than it previously was, but it is still possible. The key is to locate the sellers available to purchase the right homes at the right price, both of which you can easily do in the market of today. Flipping can still be an effective method of getting high profit, even in the present market. Now that you have armed yourself with the basics, you need to go further by learning the steps involved in the rehab process, which we will break down in the next chapter.

Chapter 2: The Renovating/Rehab Process

As we covered earlier, rehabbing a property involves the purchase of a cheap or partially deteriorated property, investing your money and time into enhancing it, and then selling it for profit.

Even though this investment is a profitable one, for new investors, it is one of the more expensive and riskier approaches for investing in real estate. A good rehab project requires capital, time, detail, and experience before you can be a pro. So, even though this is an investment strategy with a lot of potential profit, you need to be ready before you go into it. To help with this, we will look into a few steps to take when rehabbing a property.

Appraise the Investment Property

This is a step no real estate investor should ignore before they invest in a property. Get the services of an experienced home inspector, and take a walk around the property you have plans to rehabilitate. This is the most vital step to take if you plan on being successful in rehabbing properties because it will aid you in understanding what you are walking into.

The home inspection will consist of an examination of the property's electrical system, heating, roof, floor, air conditioning system, plumbing, and doors, among other things.

As you can observe, as an investor, you will need the services of an experienced home inspector to finish this step successfully. The investors, aside from being able to point out and give priority to the areas that need repair, can also notice things that you may have overlooked.

Make a Checklist

When you have a clear view of the kind of work the property needs, the next thing you will require is a checklist. You can categorize this as a list of things you need to do to finish a rehab on a property. Here, you need to put down the necessary repairs pointed out by the home inspector and create an estimate of the associated expenses.

This will function as a roadmap that shows you where you need to begin and where you need to head to from there. It will be ideal to begin with the main enhancements needed, and leave minor fixes for last.

Create a Budget

Before you purchase a property to invest in, you

need to have an estimate of the cost of repairs. Also, a budget is essential before you begin a rehab project. For this reason, the instant you understand the scope of work required, you need to develop a budget of the amount you are willing to spend on renovating the property.

While doing this, it is crucial to take note of your ROI, as you don't want to overspend on a property and not make any profit. Additionally, remember to estimate the after repair value (ARV), since you aim to make a profit when you are finished with the property. This step is essential in helping you determine if the investment property will increase in value when you are done with the rehab, so you can sell it for a higher value than the price of the purchase, in addition to the cost of renovation.

There is always a chance for unforeseen costs to come up. For this reason, you need to always to make room in your budget for these costs. Lastly, also consider the holding costs when creating your budget, in the event the property does not sell immediately.

Locate The Appropriate Contractor

Many investors choose to save costs by using inexperienced or cheap contractors. This is not the way to go, as tempting as their lower rates may be, as it usually leads to disaster in the long run. For this reason, it is important to find an experienced and trustworthy contractor with a proper license.

Even though you will spend more, the work will be of more efficient and be of better quality, which helps in adding to the amount of profit you can earn. However, not all contractors come with the same level of skill and experience, so you need to spend a lot of time researching general contractors. Ensure any contractor you choose is insured, licensed, dependable, and suits both your budget and your needs.

Get the Needed Permits

As an investor, you will need some essential permits to rehab a property. It's best to investigate the kinds of permits you need before you purchase a property, so you don't violate the building codes of your area. As a new investor, you can reach out to your local housing department to obtain information on all the necessary permits. Additionally, your contractor can help you decide the permits you have to get based on the kind of work you need to do on the property.

Also, never start a rehab until you have gotten all the necessary permits, as it could result in a loss of your investment. For instance, not having a permit to make upgrades may prevent you from being able to sell. It may also delay projects, cause issues with the housing authority, and drastically elevate your expenses, which can all have a negative impact on your profits. To prevent these things from happening, you need to be smart about your investment and get all the permits you need *before* you begin a rehab.

Rehabbing the Property

Now that you have completed the first stages, you can begin the physical process of rehabilitating the property. The steps below will help you complete a rehab on your investment property:

Begin the Cleanup Phase

The first step is to get rid of all the damaged items and trash like broken windows, doors, and any other detritus around the exterior and interior of the property. The aim of this is to clean up the property and get it ready for the process of rehabilitation, so the project progresses and runs seamlessly. This does not increase the value of the property, but it does not have to cost you anything either, as it is a task you can take on yourself.

Begin with Enhancements to The Interior

According to experts, the interior is the best place to begin. It is the place where people will reside and spend most of their time, so this is where you need to channel most of your investment. If your budget is limited, pay attention to the repairs that will offer you the most returns on your cash. Also, you can use DIY enhancements to spruce up a property's interior, which will help cut expenses.

The first step is to find the core systems in the property that need repairs. Ensure you have hired on plumbers, HVAC contractors, electricians and other professionals to help with these repairs. If you want to complete some aspects like painting on your own, it is certainly possible, but it is better to have a professional painter help out if you can spare the expense.

Lastly, you can move on to the replacement of tiles and flooring. All of these will make the property look more appealing and enhance its value.

Enhance the Exterior

After completion of the interior fixes, you can go ahead with enhancing the exterior to offer it the needed curb appeal. This could range from replacing the front door, shutters, garage door or driveway.

A few ways of enhancing the curb appeal during a property rehab is to improve the landscape, paint the front door, install new lights, mailboxes, and siding. These may seem like minor changes, but they will help increase your property's value and help make sure it feels like home to potential buyers or customers.

Finalizing Stage

Before you consider yourself done with a home rehab project, the last step is to finish up the improvements. You need to go through the changes alongside your contractor and determine if anything requires adjustment. You can also hire a professional to inspect, as they can ensure all the work done is up to standard. Then, you put up the property for rent or sale. But before you can actively engage in the house flipping business, there are a few things you need to put in place, like your financing. We will be taking a detailed look at how you can get funding for your flip in the next chapter.

Chapter 3: Get Your Financing in Place

Investing in real estate can provide you with a consistent stream of income and the opportunity to switch professions. Popular shows on television teaches us that flipping houses is not hard, and you can get the hang of it within a few days.

But the reality is a bit different. You do require the expertise and the ability to make solid plans. However, for many people who invest in real estate or plan to do so, the main challenge they deal with is that of financing. You have to spend cash to make cash. Many investors don't even get to the stage of renovating the property before running out of funds. Then they get stuck with a home they can't sell or continue working on. This is a spot you don't want to find yourself in, and that is why you need to put your financing in place beforehand.

So what available options for finances do you have at your disposal? We will be taking a comprehensive look at these below.

Getting Financing

There are two standard methods of purchasing a

home:

- You use your personal cash

- You take out a loan from someone else and pay back after you close

As an investor, your goal should be to attain the level where you will be able to pay for any flip with your own money. However, this is pricey for most first-time investors, so this is not the first option most will have.

If you are going to be taking out a loan from someone else, it is known as "financing" the deal. There are a variety of ways of borrowing cash to finance investment deals, and we will be taking a look at them later on in this chapter.

But first, there are a few things you need to put in place before you apply for loans.

Things to Put in Place Before You Apply for A House Flipping Loan

When investing in real estate, you learn on the go. The more houses you flip, the better you will begin to understand the rights and wrongs when it comes to financing.

However, before you search for financing for

house flipping, you need to understand a few things. Knowing these will speed up the process of borrowing and assure your lender that you are good for the loan.

Develop a Business Plan for Every Flip

Lenders typically do not want to loan cash to rehab homes that are not in good condition. However, you have a better perspective of the property than any other individual. It will be your duty to provide the lender with information regarding every home you want to flip.

This is why it is vital to create a business plan for your flip. It does not have to be a very long plan, but you need to put down a comprehensive evaluation of each home consisting of:

- Precise home address

- Investigation of the area where you are purchasing the home

- Sale prices for comparable houses in the area

- Plan, financial forecasts and time needed for the rehab

- Information on any individual who will aid you with the project, e.g., general contractor and partner

- Plan B in the event the renovation does not go how you want

- The present estimate of the property and projected value after repair from an experienced appraiser

- Pointing out each of these areas in your business plan will make lenders take you seriously. It will also make sure you obtain a loan large enough to cover all your expenses.

Get Accurate Estimates of All Costs of Renovation

Many flippers end up not getting enough cash from their lender. If you do not have enough money to settle with your contractors, your project may end up being stuck midway through the renovation. To avoid this issue, your best bet is to develop a broad work scope before you apply for the loan. A scope of work is an elaborate summary of all the costs, timelines, and repairs you will be carrying out in the home.

To put the scope of work in place, you will require assistance from an experienced contractor and appraiser. With their combined efforts, they will investigate comparable projects, and offer you an educated guess of timeline and cost. Before you reach out to a lender, you need to have an elaborate scope of work in place, or you would have no idea of the amount of cash you want to borrow. The scope of work will also consist of two additional numbers that are vital to lenders: the After Repair Value (ARV) and Loan to Value (LTV), which we will be taking a further look at later.

Develop Your Network

One final thing to keep in mind before you apply for your loan is that connections are vital in real estate. Become a part of the (REIA) Real Estate Investors Association or club to connect with other investors. Lots of real estate investors borrow money to finance their projects and also invest in other people's projects. In essence, the individuals you connect with could become lenders or partners in your subsequent deals.

Ways to Get Financing

Having put all these things in place and having determined the amount of money you need, you will now be able to check out your options for financing if you are going with the option of taking out a loan.

Bank Financing

The first place you may want to apply for a loan is at a bank near you. Obtaining loans from banks for flipping is just like getting any other form of mortgage loan. You will define the loan's length and place the down payment required along with any other requirements.

This might sound easy, but getting a loan from the bank to invest in your house flipping business is not without its challenges. To be eligible for the loan, you will need a good credit rating. What's more, if your history in house flipping is not a good one, the bank may not be keen on providing you with financing and could deny the loan.

Personal Loans

A personal loan is a very flexible financing option. When you get a personal loan, you can channel the money to any area you desire, which includes flipping.

To be eligible for this loan, you will likely require a credit score of more than 650. Personal loan charges can be as low as 5 percent, and you will have the capacity to clear it up in monthly installments over three to seven years. The only drawback is that the loan has a cap of $50,000. This may be barely enough for a successful flip, so you may need to merge it with other financing options.

Line of Credit

Tapping into the equity of the home you live in is another well-known option for financing a flip. However, this is only an option if you already own a home. A home equity line of credit (HELOC) or home equity loan (HEL) can offer you funding for your next flip, and you can pull in the cash you require. You will only need to pay interest on the money you utilize. Different from a loan, a line of credit allows you to borrow as high as the limit as required.

The difference between the balance of your mortgage and your home market value is your equity. To be deemed eligible for a line of credit or home equity loan, your home needs to have no less than 20 percent equity, preferably higher depending on the amount you need to borrow. It is also essential for you to have great credit and adequate monthly earnings to pay for both your mortgage and the HELOC or HEL.

Lots of banks will allow you to loan as much as 85 percent of the cost of your residence, after deducting the remainder of your loan balance. The main downside of using the financing method is that your home is being placed as collateral. If you are unable to keep up with the payments, your property can get foreclosed upon by the bank. This can be a potential risk if you plan to use the revenue from your flip to pay for your loan.

Hard Money Loan

A hard money loan is one you get from individuals or investors and not from a bank. Here, the lenders have lower requirements for you to be eligible and offer you the cash for flipping in two weeks or less. Because hard money lenders work alongside borrowers who are not as creditworthy, their rates of interest are higher, usually around 10 to 20 percent. Also, lenders include fees on the loans, which makes the overall cost much higher. This is why it is best to try out other, cheaper, options before you go with a hard money loan.

There are many online platforms and private business loan lenders who focus on providing hard money loans to house flippers. One such platform is LendingHome. There are also other hard money options where numerous investors combine their resources to provide funding for your project called crowdfunding platforms.

Hard money loans aim to keep you "above water" until you are done with renovating your home and selling it. Thus, there is a one-year term attached to the average hard money loan, even though you are open to other longer options. These loans need you to place a little down payment, which is normally around 10 percent. This is because the lender is more concerned about the property's prospects as opposed to the borrower's background.

Hard money loans work differently from other kinds of loans. Here, the lenders provide approval for your loans in segments. First, they offer you the cash for the initial purchase of the home and the initial batches of renovations. The moment the contractor is through with the primary repairs, you will be offered the cash for the subsequent set of improvements, and so on.

Loan from Family and Friends

Under normal circumstances, it is paramount that you don't combine personal relationships with loans or money in general. But, this does not mean it is a bad idea to obtain loans from your friends or loved ones. It is not as tedious as other options of financing, and there is a high possibility that you would get loans at lower interest rates in comparison to banks and hard money lenders. This is because of the personal connection your family and friends share with you.

However, there are a few fundamental rules to borrowing from friends and family. First, you need to put down the terms in writing and specifically state the rate of interest and the time required to pay the loan — a written document aids in protecting both parties. The next rule is to go with the securities laws and IRS laws that apply to family investments.

Look for a Financing Partner

Lots of investors in real estate get stuck in an infuriating situation: They possess a knowledge of the market to know when there is a good opportunity to flip but don't have adequate financing to complete the project. Bringing in a partner, however, can help. They can support you in doing the following:

- Locating the opportunity to flip

- Planning and supervision of the renovation

- Providing financing

Depending on the amount every partner invests, they get a cut in the earnings. Normally, a partner provides the funding for restoration, while the other partner locates the opportunity to flip and supervises the renovation. You may want to stick to the same partner for numerous projects or use a different one for each project.

The share the partner who provides the funds gets is dependent on their negotiation with other partners, and if they are providing support for the project in other ways. The great part of finding a financing partner is that when there is a loss instead of a profit, they also share in the loss. Similar to loans you get from family and friends, you need to put down all the conditions associated with the project using a partnership agreement.

Real Estate Crowdfunding Sites

This is another funding option which is growing more popular in providing financing for all kinds of projects, including flipping houses. The way it works is simple: Lots of people pool their resources together to support real estate projects that pique their interest.

Depending on the site used, most of the crowdfunding sources for house flipping are either developed as equity or debts. Debt funding means that investors purchase an aspect of the loan or the loan itself. Equity crowdfunding, on the other hand, means that investors buy the home being flipped.

401(k) Financing

Taking a loan or withdrawing cash from your 401(k) account is another option to get funding. However, if you are getting close to the age of retirement, this may not be the best bet. But for flippers on the young side, if the rewards are more than the risks, loaning some funds from your 401(k) may be worth it.

Lots of 401(k) accounts provided by employers, give you the chance to take loans of as much as 50 percent of your remaining balance. Self-employed individuals using solo 401(k) plans also have the capacity to get loans of as much as $50,000. This loan also requires you to pay interest, but the cash belongs to you, so the interest and principal you pay back goes to you.

Similar to this, some individuals borrow from their life insurance policy to finance their flip. If you have one, you can ask your insurance company about eligibility requirements.

Your Financial Inventory

Now that you understand the kinds of financing available to you, you need to learn about some essential things to put in place before requesting a loan. Similar to applying for a job that pays well, you will need to be ready when asking people to invest in your business.

Although it is not compulsory for you to put it all down in writing, there are some vital elements of your financial position that you have to prepare in advance. This would be useful during discussions with any individual who wants to fund your investment.

These are the components that normally define the kinds of financing you can get. This means it is crucial for you to take a realistic stock of where you are before you begin to request money from anyone.

The following are aspects of your financial resume your lenders will be concerned about:

Credit Score/Credit History

You need to know your credit score and credit history. If you want to get financing for your projects, good credit is vital. If you have no idea what your credit score is, or you just want to check out your credit history, click here for a free copy. Lots of lenders will begin the process of underwriting by reviewing your credit score. It needs to be over 650 to be great, and if it is not, they may not be too keen on providing you with financing, or if they do, it may be at high interest rates.

This does not imply there are no other options available to you, but by paying attention to developing a good credit score and history, you will have access to the majority of the options for finance available.

Your Earnings

Your income is the next important part of your financial condition. Are you presently doing something to generate consistent income? Do you have a rental property generating money monthly? Lenders will look into all of these sources of income to determine if you will be able to pay back the lines of credit or loans they provide to you.

Your earnings and the longer the time you have had it coming will make lenders more interested in offering you cash. From their point of view, if you have substantial earnings alongside your investment, you will be in a better position to repay loans if the investment does not work out. Similar to credit score, if you have no recurrent earnings, you are still privy to a lot of options even if they are not as much.

Your Resources

Your assets are another vital aspect of your financial condition lenders will take a look at. Providing answers to these questions will be critical:

- Do you have money saved up?

- Do you have landed property or have sufficient equity on your properties?

- Do you have a large retirement fund?

- Do you have other assets you could sell off to settle with lenders in case your investment fails to pay off?

In many situations, lenders will consider loaning

you cash if you own assets that you are keen on placing as collateral against the loan. This implies that, if you fail to pay back the loan, the lender takes over the asset instead. For instance, if your home has a decent amount of equity, the lender may request that you place your home as collateral for loans. If you are unable to pay back the loan for any reason, the lender takes over your home.

Debt

Do you presently have any other credit obligations? The truth is, the higher the amount of money you owe, the harder it would be to obtain financing. Sadly, this is something investors in real estate, even those who are already established, must deal with.

There are various kinds of debts, and some are not as bad as others. Any existing liability is going to hamper your ability to pay back extra loans and would reduce the possibility of you getting financing for your flip. Specifically, lenders will check out your income to debt ratio. If your income is way higher than your debts, it means you will be left with more money after each month, and you are more likely to pay back.

Familiarity with Investing

This does not have to do with your finance, but lenders would have an interest in your investment experience. An investor who has had lots of success in investment is more likely to pay back a loan as opposed to one without any experience at all. Having a great business plan can serve as an excellent replacement for experience. Lenders will ignore the absence of experience if you have a clear direction and a detailed plan in place.

As you attain experience, your options for financing will become more copious. But for now, ensure you have at least developed a great business plan, set clear goals, and a means of achieving them. Having determined how you will get your financing, the next thing you have to do is to locate a good agent. This is what we will cover in the next chapter.

Chapter 4: Locate Your Agent(s)

Flipping houses may seem like an easy and fun way to make quick cash on a real estate investment; however, flipping homes is not quite so straightforward in practice. Purchasing, remodeling, and selling a home within a brief time period, while making a profit along the way, is an enormous task even for the most experienced real estate investors.

Fortunately, you don't have to handle this job by yourself. Hiring a real estate agent who is knowledgeable and skilled in flipping homes to help you out can help you save money, time, and hassles during the process.

Collaborating with an agent who is versed in flipping houses can offer you a range of benefits in all phases of the transactions. Agents can aid you in:

- Understanding the conditions of the present market and your local housing market.

- Go through properties and locate the appropriate buyers

- Decide the proper remodeling projects and find great contractors

- Determine the appropriate list price

Is Your Housing Market Suitable for Flipping Houses?

A local agent with the right experience can aid you in determining whether it is a wise investment for you to flip. Despite popular belief, flipping is not a great idea in all cities. This means, if the conditions of the real estate market in your area are not promising, you won't make a substantial profit on your investment.

And even if your location is not presently the greatest for house flipping, it does not mean things won't change later. The conditions of the real estate market are continuously evolving, due to a range of factors like increasing rates of mortgage and varying rates of inventory. An experienced agent will have the ability to discern the details of your local market.

An Agent Can Locate the Appropriate House for You

House flipping is an uncertain investment that does not provide you with any assurances. You are taking a risk that a home will sell for a higher amount if you spend a certain amount of cash on upgrades and repairs.

So, when making your financial plans, you need to

make estimates on the possible value of resale and unforeseen expenses which are typical during a renovation. If you don't get these numbers right, you may not make any profit. Newbies in the flipping business often end up investing too much in a home they want to flip. The higher the amount you pay for the property, the lower the cash available for the remodel. The higher the costs of remodeling and purchasing the home, the lower your profit margins.

Locating the appropriate home to flip is one of the most critical decisions you will make all through the process. Active agents with knowledge of the present market will be knowledgeable in the information you need to aid you in making the right purchase that will let you stay within your budget. Your agent is also your top bet to determine whether the remodel fees will suit your budget or not.

The home's current condition is a core factor in determining which as-is home to buy. It has to have depreciated enough for the seller to receive a bargain, but also be in good enough condition that you can afford to get it fixed. Your agent will also evaluate the surroundings and determine: Are the values of home in your environment declining? Is your home in a growing neighborhood? These are questions agents will investigate before they offer you as-is homes to choose from.

Lastly, an agent can help you figure out the amount of cash you can afford to invest when fixing a home. When making a financial plan, there are a range of numbers you need to consider, which an agent can effectively help you with.

An Agent Offers You Market-Driving Tips When Remodeling

The business of flipping homes comes with a lot of expenses. You can't make renovations like you plan on living in the home or you won't make good returns. You need to answer the following questions:

- Is this going to earn me cash?

- Am I just flushing money down the drain that won't yield me any returns?

The idea is to understand that wise remodeling choices don't mean you need to buy the most expensive materials. When upgrading the kitchen cabinet of your home, you may want to spend huge cash on well-known brand sinks. But when you are flipping a house, going with a brand that is less pricey would also work. You will also be able to save money on these extra expenses.

Agents who have experience in flipping can help you find the best bulk deals to help you save cost.

Some agents have direct connections with manufacturers to buy old inventory at a reduced price, or from contractors who have leftover materials from a housing development they have completed.

An Agent Offers You Advise On When-to-Sell

On paper, all houses have a projected value. However, when the moment comes to sell, it is only valued at what the buyer is interested in paying and what the bank is prepared to finance.

An agent who has experience in flipping pays attention to market trends during the process of remodeling to aid their seller in setting the appropriate list price during the right moment. Along with evaluating the value added with the remodel, your agent will consider your expenses to make sure you can get back your investment while making a decent profit as well.

However, there are times when you may be advised by an agent to hold onto the property for some months, or perhaps rent it out for some time, to ensure you have a better chance of earning a higher profit – or ensuring you don't lose cash on the deal. Don't forget that the market conditions of the real estate market are continuously changing and may even change before you finish remodeling.

And if the value of the home falls before you can flip, it may be a good idea to hold on until there is an improvement in the market conditions. When dips like these take place, flippers who do not have a knowledgeable agent by their side can end up selling at a loss.

Newbies to the business of house flipping frequently miscalculate the amount of cash it requires to flip a home, and the level of risk it comes with. However, if you collaborate with a knowledgeable agent, you will be able to make sure that your first flip is a great success.

What Kind of Agent Should You Choose?

The first thing you need to consider is: Are you purchasing or selling a home? Your response here is what will determine the kind of agent you need to work with. Agents who work alongside homeowners who want to sell a home are known as listing agents or seller's agents. These agents act in your interest as a homeowner during the process of listing and negotiation.

Agents who work with individuals who want to buy a home are known as selling agents or buyer's agents. These agents act on behalf of buyers during the process of showing and negotiation. There are a few buyer's agents who work with buyers alone. This means they don't list any houses for sellers whatsoever.

Many individuals in the home selling and buying processes are often confused by the terms selling agent and seller's agent because they sound similar. But, they act on behalf of various parties with unique interests. Selling agents act on behalf of the party purchasing the home, but they only become selling agents after signing of the final contract. On the other hand, seller's agents act on behalf of individuals who want to sell a home. There are also agents who act in the interests of both buyers and sellers. They are called dual agents.

Dual Agents

These agents act on behalf of the seller's and the buyer's interests during the process of purchasing homes. The way it works is simple. Picture yourself going into a home for sale and falling for the location immediately. You know the property is a hot one and won't stay long on the market. You just began to look for a home and have no agent yet. But the listing agent is on the property and is ready to assist you with an offer right at that moment. You don't want to hold off while you find an agent of your own, so you choose to work with him. In this situation, you just got into a functional affiliation with a dual agent.

There is a lot of debate surrounding dual agency because agents will have to remain neutral and work cautiously all throughout the process. After all, they are representing a buyer who wants the least price for a home and a seller who is looking to get the most they can, all for the same home.

Also, in terms of commission, there may be a possible conflict of interest. During a standard sale, the listing agent and buyer's agent share the commission equally. However, dual agents get to keep the entire commission, which implies selling a home for the highest price possible works in their favor. This turns out well for the seller but not so much for the buyer.

Lots of experts in real estate have strong feelings against dual agency, and this is not without good reason. Dual agents are not permitted by law to choose sides in the transaction or share private information. In essence, they get twice the commission while offering less direction and advice to both parties. The majority of the time, only the agent gets any real benefit from this transaction.

Dual agency is not allowed in all states, but it is lawful in some states, like Texas and California. In the states where it is authorized, agents are bound by law to reveal their dual agency before anyone signs a contract. To determine whether or not your state supports dual agency, you need to run a Google search along the lines of: "Is dual agency legal in" along with the name of your state. Having decided the kind of agent you need, the next thing you need to figure out is how to choose that agent.

How to Choose a House Flipping Agent

Choosing the right agent is of critical importance. But what makes a good agent?

There are a few characteristics to look out for which can help you with that. We will be discussing these characteristics below:

Experience

Would you want a surgeon without experience to do a life-saving operation on you? I am guessing the answer is no. The experience a surgeon obtains when practicing their expertise is priceless, and the same applies to real estate agents.

You don't want an agent without any practical experience. You want to look for one who understands how to list and sell homes, the buying process, is familiar with their local market and one who has access to the MLS.

Contrary to popular belief, you don't need someone

with specific experience in house flipping. What you do need is someone who comprehends the peaks and valleys of real estate itself. You need to go with an agent whose skill level you are comfortable with – one who understands what they are doing and has solid past experience doing it.

Has Time for You

Believe it or not, when looking for an agent, you don't want to go with the best real estate agent in the district. The agent with their picture on every bench or billboard will not have adequate time to invest in your business. If an agent already has a considerable volume of business and is already deep-rooted in their field, they are more challenging to teach, because they are already used to how they do things. If they have not collaborated with investors before, it can be a difficult task to help them understand your goals from a house flipper's perspective.

Avoid individuals like these and search for agents that are not as popular and established. These kinds of agents will be more eager to collaborate with you and invest the time to learn what you want. They will also be able to provide you with the level of attention you need and deserve.

Devoted to their Job

Focus is essential, and you will want to pick an agent who is focused on what they do and dedicated to ensuring their business works. A flying instructor who works on the side, showing homes, is not the person you want. Look for an agent who is into this as their full-time job, because you will need their complete attention when the process kicks off.

Inspired by Relationships

Many of us work together in business to make money. However, the commission an agent earns should not be the core motivation behind them collaborating with you. When an agent begins giving priority to the commission over the significance of developing a relationship with their partners and clients, then you may no longer be certain your best interest is what they have in mind.

Search for an agent who is inspired by the kinds of relationships they develop with those they work alongside - those who honestly want to aid their customers and work in hand with them to develop a better future. If your agent is helping you look for deals, you have to be sure that their focus is on those deals, and not the commission they will get after the property has been purchased or sold.

Capable of Learning

Similar to locating an individual who has your time, you need to ensure they can learn and are keen on doing so. Any agent who believes he knows everything would not be open to the information you offer them. And because agents don't finish the licensing test with an in-depth knowledge of evaluating properties to flip and calculating ARV, there will be a lot of things you need to share with them.

The agent's capacity to take helpful criticism is key. Those who are open to learning and eager to improve should have the ability to accept it if you tell them they are wrong. They should understand you are not dishing out insults, but are ensuring you both can make more cash at the end of the process. If you would rather represent yourself and save some money in the process, you can do so by getting a real estate license. We will cover how to do this below.

How to Get Your Real Estate License

If you have plans to get your real estate license, you will have to complete the required real estate education in your state. With this kind of education, you will be able to attain some understanding of the financial and legal aspects of real estate dealings. However, you need to note that this information would not be of much practical help for flipping homes.

One of the main benefits of getting a real estate license is being able to access the MLS. It is an unquestionable way to save lots of cash when purchasing homes to invest in. Even if the property is worth $100,000, you can easily save as much as $3,000. With your real estate license, you will have the capacity to list your properties on MLS for free. The MLS has been recognized for selling about 80 percent of sold properties, which is much higher than other kinds of marketing when it comes to house flipping.

The great news is that you will be able to benefit from both ends. You will be able to enjoy the benefits of having a license in real estate without sustaining the additional burden and access to savings. For starters, the moment you have attained your real estate license, agents will be able to legally pay you referral fees when you are flipping homes.

This implies that you can task another licensed agent with doing the work, and have them pay you back a considerable chunk of the commission they get. This offers you more returns and can provide you with extra advance cash when flipping houses. Better still, you can go with the option of hiring virtual assistants who utilize your access to carry out the daily jobs that have to be done when flipping homes. They will have the capacity to do all tasks, including reviewing contracts, uploading listings, and locating properties.

What Can You Use a Real Estate License for?

If you make the choice of getting a real estate license, you will gain access to a field of possibilities. Below are some of the possibilities that come with having a real estate license:

- **Sales Agent**: When you have a real estate license, you will have the ability to aid others in the purchase and sales of properties.

- **Leasing Agent:** Agents also can act as property managers or leasing agents for residential and commercial properties.

- **Broker**: Real estate brokers can manage and license real estate agents of their own.

Is it Compulsory to get a Real Estate License to Flip Homes?

Getting a real estate license for house flipping can be ideal, but only if it benefits you and your business in terms of flipping homes. To go into the business of flipping houses, it is not compulsory to get a real estate license.

Benefits of Having Your Real Estate License as A Rehabber

If you have plans to get your real estate license while in the house flipping business, take a look at some of the benefits you stand to gain:

- **Access to Deals:** With a real estate license, you will have the capacity to access deals you would typically not have known about. Yes, you will be able to access those available on the MLS, but there are also a range of other outlets available. When a new deal is open, you will be one of the first to know; no more waiting for an agent to reach out to you. Sometimes the promptness of execution that comes with having a license is what you need to locate a new deal.

- **New Contacts**: Having a license will expose you to networking events you may not otherwise have been aware of. Real estate is a business that has to do with people and will continue to be. With a license, you will be able to come across people of like mind and locate new deals along the way.

- **Additional Revenue:** With a real estate license, you can earn cash as a real estate agent while investing in real estate yourself. Getting a real estate license is a fantastic way to complement the revenue you are already bringing in from flipping homes. You can channel the subsequent commission you get into your next flip and make so much more.

- **Access to Commissions**: With a license, you will be able to save cash on commissions that usually go to agents in each deal. Real estate commission is often around 2.5 – 3 percent. This means on a purchase of $100,000, you are looking to earn approximately $2,500-$3,000, which would otherwise be paid to your agent. If *you* are the agent on a transaction, this money comes to you, and you can channel it to other areas.

- **Education**: To become licensed, there are certain educational conditions you must meet. However, the industry itself can help you learn a lot. The experience you get from here is adequate to get you through your career in home flipping.

As you can see, there are many benefits to attaining a real estate license. If you are keen on investing the cash and time it takes to get a license, and are prepared to exploit all the benefits that come with being a real estate agent, then it is probably an ideal choice for you. Once you have determined the type of agent you need, or if you have instead decided to get your license, the next step is to decide where to buy your property. The next chapter will take a more in-depth look at this.

Chapter 5: Where You Should Buy?

One of the most vital decisions many newbies in the house flipping business have issues with is where to invest. Investing in the wrong location can result in a massive amount of losses down the road. For this reason, it is essential for you to do thorough investigations before you choose a place to buy.

The buying area of an investor is called their *farm area*, which could be as large as a metro area or as little as one neighborhood. Clearly, the smaller the farm area, the easier it would be for you to know it and the houses within it. However, the bigger the farm area, the more opportunities available to locate incredible deals. How do you determine the right farm area for you?

How to Choose the Right Real Estate Farm Area

Because it can require a considerable amount of time to get high returns from your farm area, the choice you make is critical. Here are a few steps to choosing a profitable farm area for real estate:

Choose a Farm Area Close to Home

If you are just beginning, it may be a great choice to

farm your own area. By utilizing a community networking platform, you will be able to position yourself as the real estate expert for the job in a specific area. There are lots of advantages of farming in the area you live which include:

- **You are an Expert in your Location**: By creating your farm area in an environment you already know about and love is the best combination possible. You know the surroundings and many of the inhabitants, and you also have knowledge that would not be easy for non-residents to learn. For instance, you may know a friend of your neighbor who is moving and wants to sell his home soon. In addition to offering fantastic service, you will also be one of the first to know the things happening in the market. A lot of individuals already know you, so it would be less complicated for you to establish business and trust in contrast to a newcomer. Even if you are a new resident in the neighborhood, it is less difficult to make contacts in areas you already reside in. You can prove yourself as a professional in a variety of ways, including hosting local events related to real estate.

- **You Already Have the Contacts**: As someone who resides in an area, there is a possibility that you already have reliable contacts in your farm area. Your friends, family, and people you know are likely close-by. You may already know the owners of local businesses, and you can genuinely recommend the neighborhood to buyers because that is where you live. There are lots of benefits of farming in the area you live in. It is a secure method of drawing in buyers, especially those who are relocating. Consider this for a few seconds: if you just moved to a new area, would you rather collaborate with an agent who resides a few cities away or one who lives or has lived in the area for many years?

- **You Are More Accessible to Customers**: When you reside in the neighborhood you farm, there are prospects to meet potential clients while engaging in your daily activities. Locations like the coffee shop, local gym, hardware stores, and grocery stores all create great opportunities to get new contacts during everyday conversations while engaging in your usual routine. Many times, daily interactions at the mall can transform into great leads. Another reason to keep your farm area close to home is that you will have a better ability to provide previews and showings at the last minute. It is less complicated for you to show potential buyers a fantastic listing that just opened up if it is not far from where you live. It is also less challenging to manage your life and has less impact on your budget. Fees spent on gasoline and vehicle maintenance can be one of the highest expenses for a real estate agent. However, you can drastically reduce these expenses if your farm area is not far from home. In addition to picking a location close to home, it is also vital for you to carry out thorough research on your farm area.

Staying close to home is a brilliant choice; however, you need to do due diligence on your farm area before you make your final decision.

Investigate Your Farm Area

When choosing the appropriate area to farm, doing a thorough investigation is also crucial. Before you begin farming in a particular area, it is ideal for you to get as much information as you can about that area. This will ensure you are confident it is a location you will be glad to work in and offer you the revenue you require to meet your real estate business goals.

In the long run, the demographic elements are one of the aspects you should investigate in the farm area you choose. Below are a few areas to investigate:

- Average age

- Average earnings

- Is it a commuter environment?

- Are there large-scale employers like factories, hospitals, etc.?

- Are there options for transportation?

- Does it have local amenities like nightlife, malls or parks?

- Recent changes

You can get informed about many of these just by running a Google search. However, to attain the age and incomes, you will need to use census data. This data can help direct you to the types of houses people may be looking for, the types of facilities they may have an interest in and the amounts of commission checks you can anticipate. When carrying out your investigation, pay attention to all parts of the neighborhood you respond to personally. For instance, if you are a lover of new developments, it will be less difficult to sell them as opposed to old homes. Because purchasing a house is a decision that is based on emotion as much as finances, buyers are more likely to be responsive to your in-depth knowledge of the subject.

When you select a farm area, you may need to narrow it down to a precise demographic you want to work alongside in that area, which is often called *demographic farming*. For example, you may want to emphasize the houses that have a value of over $2 million. Investigating the local demographics and neighborhood will aid you in choosing an option that is suitable for you. Also, do not forget to consider boundaries when choosing a farm area, as it can help in marketing.

Pick a Farm Area with Clear Boundaries

When you can, make an effort to choose a neighborhood with clearly defined boundaries to aid in marketing your listings. If you have clearly defined limits when farming in real estate, it becomes easier to market your listings. This is because the geographic location you work is defined to others and yourself. Even in large, sprawling areas there are clearly-defined boundaries.

People foresee a specific way of life and home with labeled neighborhoods. Almost every neighborhood in any location has a specific reputation, and exploiting that reputation can aid you in marketing your listings. In addition to boundaries, the size of your farm area is something that must not be overlooked.

Ensure Your Farming Area Is the Appropriate Size

Size is of importance when it comes to geographic farming. You have to make sure the area is vast enough to get reasonable profits, but small enough that you can become an authority without exhausting all your savings. Regardless of where you reside, put the size of your neighborhood into consideration when farming in real estate. The plans you make beforehand will help you save money, time, and make sure you have a significant influx of clients for a long time to come. You could pick the largest farm area you can find, but if the numbers are not right, you will never see success.

Check your Farm Area's Numbers

The moment you locate an environment you want to farm in, the next thing you need to do is run the numbers to ensure the area has adequate sales activity to make your farming profitable. Ideally, you want to pick a farm area with high turnover, sales prices, and low level of competition. However, in reality, it is tough to locate regions like these. To be on the safe side, you may want to search numerous areas and choose the one which is well balanced as regard competition, profit, and price. Check out how to do this below.

- Average Sales Price: It is not as difficult as you may believe to determine the average sales price in your projected farm area, and you only need to take a few steps to do it. First, start up your MLS program and select the area's zip code. You can also use a program like RPR or Realtors Property Resource, as they all provide you with the ability to outline a region on the map.

To determine the average sales price, you need to draw your projected farm area on the map. Next, get all the sold listings for the last two years or more. The average price of the sold houses will be your average sale price. Once you have the average price, you can determine the commission you will get for each transaction. Then, you can decide the number of listings you will need to sell in your farm area to get returns and achieve your set goals.

● Rate of Turnover: To determine this, all you need is to divide the number of houses in your chosen farm area by the number of sold homes in the past two years. Ideally, your chosen farm area should have a reasonably high rate of turnover.

● Competition: After determining that the area has adequate sales activity to keep you going, the next thing you need to get a feel for your competition. Be sure to take note of the leading closing agents for the last two years or more. If you see that a particular agent is already dominating the market in that region, it may be difficult for you to make a move into the market. There would be a major possibility that the agent has been doing work in the area for a long time and is already an authority. On the other hand, if you observe that there are numerous agents making sales in the region, and the turnover is adequate to validate working there, then there is probably a sufficient market for you as well.

Piecing It All Together

Now that you understand everything about the area's demographics, facilities, and types of home available, the numbers regarding turnover, sales activity and competition, you need to combine that information to pick the farm area that is right for you.

When evaluating your farm area for real estate, make decisions using your data. Utilizing a formula to put the numbers together can help you remain confident that pooling your resources in this area won't be a waste of funds. It is unfortunate to get emotionally attached to a region only to discover there is no place for you to develop your flipping business. By doing a good analysis, you can avoid making this costly error in the first place. After choosing a farm area, the next step is to start developing a name for yourself in that location.

How to Develop Authority in Your Farm Area for Real Estate

Here, your objective is to assert yourself as the go-to expert in real estate for the whole community. Let's discuss a few methods of establishing your presence in your chosen farm area:

Direct Mail

This is one of the most efficient and time-tested ways of spreading your message to a precise area. You can take advantage of the EDDM or Every Door Direct Mail service offered by the US Postal Service, which lets you send mailers to every individual in your farm area even if you have no mailing list. If EDDM is new to you, it is a targeted and cost-efficient direct mail service offered by the USPS. It gives you the chance to pick a path for delivering mail through their maps, and then you will have the ability to send your direct mail to each home on that path. The key to remaining in the thoughts of all individuals in your farm area is to reach out to them numerous times. You should be prepared for no less than two mailings before you can expect a response.

Knocking on Doors

If you can handle it, knocking on doors is a fantastic way of familiarizing yourself with homeowners in your chosen farm area. It is free, as all you need is the zeal to create connections with people and some comfortable walking shoes.

One of the great parts about knocking on doors is that you can never tell where the direction of the conversation will go, and in this digital era, it is a way of getting face-to-face with individuals. Lots of people run their advertisements on the internet, and for the right kind of individual, a personal campaign helps you stand apart from the competition.

Door knocking can be a bit daunting, but it is a leading strategy for building authority in a new area. However, if you prefer something less intimidating, door hangers can be an option to look into.

Door Hangers

Using door hangers is another tried and trusted method of reaching owners of homes in your farm area. Door hangers function so well because as opposed to a postcard, which can get mixed up and abandoned in the mail, homeowners need to take off the door hanger physically before heading into their home.

Facebook Advertising

Facebook is an efficient advertising platform for those who are focused on real estate. With Facebook, you can target using zip codes and a range of other benchmarks like income, recent job, and interests, among others.

There is an excellent volume of data available for you on Facebook to capitalize on and locate your target audience. There is a "ready to move" category which consists of individuals whose online conduct is consistent with those who are ready to relocate. You can take advantage of this to find the right clients in your farm area.

Take Part in Online Local Forums

Taking part in online forums devoted to your chosen farm area is another ideal method of developing trust there. Sometimes, the best way to build trust is to take part as a regular citizen who also works as a real estate agent.

Look for the platforms your farm area have online gatherings and become a part of the conversation. Search for neighborhood subreddits, Patch sites, city data forums, and Facebook groups. Make contributions to the discussion and drop in a listing frequently, and keep in mind that anytime you relate with others, you are representing your business too.

Meetup Groups and Local Events

Local events and Meetup groups are arguably some of the best methods of creating connections to individuals in your farm area. Give priority to being social and let business come next. Help raise funds for your local rescue organization or a new pool in the community.

Genuinely take part in the area you love, and the rewards will come in droves. The moment they know who you are, they will find you in search of the services you render. Take pictures you love and post them on your online platforms, and use those moments you connect with the community to show your genuine self. Search for events you will enjoy taking part in like charity events, fairs, sales, or anywhere else the community assembles.

Get Your Website Ranked on Google Using Local Search Terms

If you are new to the business of flipping houses or real estate in general, you will undoubtedly need a website. Agents without any online presence are losing out on business and relevance as society becomes more digital, so make sure you position yourself where clients are looking.

Google is a great tool to aid you in remaining in the minds of people in your farm area. For instance, assuming your farm area is Wicker Park in Chicago. If you incorporate the words "Wicker Park" in the URL of your website, you will show up on more Google searches for the neighborhood. Something like "Wickerparkhomes.com" will draw you nearer to the first page of search results.

Real estate farming is a tested means of becoming an expert in your location and closing more sales. If you invest the time to do comprehensive research on your farm area before you spend any money, it will ensure you reap lots of rewards down the road. While at the start, this may seem like a huge task to carry out, but the tips we discussed in this chapter can help you become the go-to real estate expert in your farm area. Having figured out a suitable farm area for your real estate transactions, the next step is to decide who you should buy from. We will learn this in the next chapter.

Chapter 6: Who Should You Buy From?

Who you buy real estate from is as vital as all the other aspects of house flipping we have covered thus far. In this chapter, we will be taking a look at some of the best strategies you can use for investment in real estate. There are typically five kinds of scenarios you should focus on when investing.

They include:

- Owners with equity

- Absentee owners with equity

- Owners without equity

- Bank-owned foreclosures

- Properties at auction

Buying from Owners with Equity

Sometimes, homeowners deal with personal issues which may compel them to let go of their properties at a reduced rate. Some of the major reasons for this include financial distress, death, relocation, and divorce.

It may be hard to purchase from sellers dealing

with financial problems because the mortgage they owe could be way beyond the worth of their property. This means they are unable to sell at a reasonable price and afford to pay off their mortgage simultaneously.

However, in other situations, the homeowners are in haste to sell and don't owe so much on their mortgage, which means they can sell to you at a reasonably decent price and still pay off their mortgage – they have equity in their home. When a homeowner in distress has equity on their property, it means there is an amazing chance for you to come in and aid the homeowner out of this issue while ensuring you get a great deal which will make you profit down the road. Here, everyone wins.

Buying from Absentee Owners with Equity

When you come across the phrase "absentee owners," it usually refers to landlords. In a few situations, these are homeowners who have become landlords due to circumstance. For some, they inherited a home which they had issues selling off and rented it out for the time being. Others may have relocated to another geographic area.

In other situations, these are investors who bought the property for the sole purpose of making money from it through rent. All of these scenarios can offer you profitable deals.

Buying from Owners Without Equity

Many investors or homeowners who are dealing with issues on their property may go with a short sale. A short sale is a unique form of purchase straight from the owner of a home whose debt on his loan is higher than the value of this property and is having a hard time meeting their mortgage payment. The process of a short sale begins when the owner of the home, who is having issues making their mortgage payment, authorizes their lender (which could be the bank or other lenders) to sell their home at a value below the amount they owe as a mortgage.

Most times, the bank would instead choose to go with a short sale than a foreclosure because the process of foreclosure does not come cheap. Lots of money and time is invested into it, and the bank may end up selling for much less than they got from the short sale. In the end, the short sale is a win for all parties involved.

Buying Foreclosures at Auction

If you are an experienced investor, this could provide you access to lots of great deals, but as a new investor, it might not be a great option. The reason is, you need to invest a lot of time into your due diligence, and skipping even a small aspect of it could lead to severe financial losses down the road.

When you purchase a property using this method, all the liens, claims, and debts associated with the property become yours. However, this does not mean you can't find great deals via auctions.

Buying (REO) Bank-Owned Foreclosures

REO properties are those have passed through the process of foreclosure, and nobody was interested in buying at the auction, and now, the bank is going through a typical sales process in real estate, in a bid to dispose of the property. A licensed real estate agent helps in listing the property on the MLS, and people who are interested in buying turn in their offers the same way they would at other properties.

The asset manager, whose role is to supervise the sale of the REO properties, will review the offers. They have the power to reject or accept offers made on the property. If the asset manager accepts an offer, a leading official in the bank makes the final approval. After approval of a sale, and contracts have been signed, the property goes through the usual closing process which takes around 3-6 weeks to complete.

Choosing the Best Option for You

When determining the situations and sellers that

will be ideal for you, consider the following:

- **Your disposition**. Are you the kind of person who loves talking to people? Are you understanding enough to place yourself in the trying shoes of the sellers? If yes, it could be a great choice to work with owners. If this is not the case, you may want to go with other options where the sellers are corporations and not homeowners. When choosing a seller to do business with, it is vital to consider your personality and how it could affect your business.

- **What is your timescale?** Do you want a project that could span a few months before you close or one that you can close fast? If time is not vital to you, then you can go for a short sale or REO. If you want something quicker, you can purchase a property at an auction. Your timescales also play a major role in helping you choose a seller.

- **Where you are situated**? Do you reside in a location that has numerous homeowners with equity? If yes, aiming at homeowners in distress or reluctant landlords can bring you fantastic leads. Are there plenty of short sale deals and REO on your MLS? If yes, this may be an avenue to exploit. The area you are located in and its present real estate market will have huge roles to play when targeting sellers.

After you figure out who you will buy from and which seller is best for you, the next thing you have to do is learn how you can find the best deals, which we will explore in the following chapter.

Chapter 7: How to Locate the Best Deals

At this point, you understand your financing options, and you know how to find your agent. Also, you already know where to buy and who to buy from. But how do you find the properties that suit your requirements? You can go about it via numerous ways which we will be discussing in this chapter.

Use the MLS

The MLS (Multiple Listing Service) is a databank assembled by real estate brokers. It lists all the properties for sale in a geographical location, together with the properties' features and other essential information. The MLS can only be assessed by licensed real estate agents. As previously discussed, this is one of the major benefits you stand to gain if you get licensed. However, if you have not been licensed, another great way of gaining access is to collaborate with a licensed agent. This could take the form of a favor, business partner, or team member. If you are hiring a real estate agent for your project, make sure they can access the MLS.

Taking advantage of the MLS to locate good flip deals offers some benefits in making the right home purchase. For one, the majority of the properties to be sold in a location are listed in one area. Additionally, the listings tend to come alongside other useful information as compared with what you can find on other platforms. If you want to purchase a property to flip and you have no way to access the MLS, there are other platforms you could try out. Sites like Realtor.com and Zillow.com offer you comprehensive information on properties for sale in a given location. However, the information may not be as in-depth as what you can find on the MLS listings.

Become a Part of a Real Estate Investment Group

During the past few years, real estate investment groups have become more recognized. There is a chance you have a few around you, and it may be an excellent idea to try them out. These groups can provide you education and networking prospects that may be significant when in search of a property to flip. Additionally, these groups usually show real estate listings on their sites and in their newsletters.

You can find a lot of these groups on social media platforms like Facebook and LinkedIn. A lot of these groups offer you assess to meetups and conferences, which will provide you the chance to meet with prospective sellers of properties and investors in person.

Search for Auctions

Auctions are great places for you to check if you have cash available to purchase the home. There are a lot of places you can look at for great properties such as a sheriff's sale, estate auction or private auction. Many regions list the properties for foreclosure numerous weeks before the sale takes place. Estate auctions and private auctions are also typically publicized weeks ahead of time. By going through these lists, you have the opportunity to look at a property before its sale date. However, you can only check out the property from far off and won't be able to go closer for a more detailed look.

However, there is a chance of becoming too involved with the bidding when purchasing properties at a live auction. Many bidders do not remember their plans before the auction and fall into the trap of bidding higher than they originally budgeted for. If you are in a bidding war with other buyers for a property, create a limit for yourself and follow it.

Purchasing through an auction also comes with another hazard. Many auctioneers will ask that you pay a fee in advance before you win a bid. This fee is usually 10 percent of the property's purchase price. It will also be mandatory for you to complete the payment within 30 days of the auction date. If you fail to complete the payment, you will have to let go of the deposit. As a result, this method is not ideal for those who don't like risks. If you want a less risky option, you can try speaking to a wholesaler.

Talk to Wholesalers

Wholesalers deal in locating properties for rehab, placing them under contract and then finding a buyer who will perform the house flip. The buyer replaces the wholesaler in the contract and pays the fee to the wholesaler for being the intermediary.

Although this is not the most budget-friendly method of finding deals, it will ensure you save time and money going forward. Many wholesalers are very engaged in what they do and have lots of connections in specific areas.

Use Classifieds

The use of daily newspapers for the sale of properties was once popular. Unfortunately, this is no longer the case as recognition of print media keeps dwindling with the rise of technology and the convenience that comes along with it. Many newspapers still run classified ads, but for many investors, this is not on the top of their list.

This is not without good reason. It can be hectic to

search through ads listed in a newspaper. You also do not have the capacity to search using a specific category or feature and the downsides outweigh the benefits. If you want something convenient, and less tasking, using an agent would be a better option.

Find an Agent

If you don't know an area too well, you can add an agent to your team. Hiring an agent is an efficient way of getting a rehab property. Agents will have insight into the best locations for flipping, and this offers them the ability to screen the opportunities available to you. They will also have the ability to offer you supplementary advice on investing for your house flip.

Getting the services of an agent who focuses on REO can also be an effective method of finding great deals. REO stands for "real estate owned," and refers to properties claimed by lenders when owners are unable to make their loan payments. A lot of these homes will have already had a foreclosure process, and possibly an eviction process.

Also, the past owners of the homes may not have invested in caring for and maintaining the property while the foreclosure was ongoing. As a result, you can get these properties way beyond the market value, which is why they are ideal for flipping. Lots of lenders have connections with a few real estate agents that deal in selling these types of properties. Locating them is easy, as all you need to do is collaborate with an agent who has access to new homes available for rehab on the market.

Use a Short Sale

When homeowners are unable to pay their mortgages, they may be offered the opportunity of selling the home "short" by the bank. This means the owner sells the home for less than the value they owe on the mortgage. Many banks prefer this option to foreclosure because of how pricey and consuming it is to sell properties that have been foreclosed upon. Short sales could create an excellent opening for you as a buyer to purchase properties from homeowners who want to let go of the property quickly.

Buying a property via a short sale also comes with its downsides. For one, it takes a larger amount of time to finish the transaction, as opposed to a typical sale. The reason is because the short sale, and its price, require the lender's approval. What's more, lenders who agree to this hardly ever pay for any extra fees that a typical seller usually makes. What this means is that you could be faced with additional closing costs. You can speak to a real estate agent to find out more about short sale listings.

Use REO

When a home gets foreclosed in an auction, the bank or lender will become the new owner. These properties are classified as real estate owned listings or REO. Many banks are happy to let go of REO properties to clear up their accounts, and this means you are probably going to find it at a lower price. Some lenders send listings for REO properties through emails or newsletters. But, you can contact your local banks to find out if they have properties to dispose of. However, before you buy, be cautious of severe property damage and liens before making the purchase.

Seller Direct

When the cost of properties are at their peak and the market is buoyant, it may not be easy to find flipping deals. Sometimes, you may be unable to pinpoint these deals because the seller has not yet made the decision to sell their property. Seller direct means getting across to homeowners at strategic moments, like the period before they list their properties, and make them an irresistible offer on their home before it hits the market. There are a lot of tools that use public data to outline tendency-to-sell models. If you want a more conventional option, taking a drive around can be what you need.

Take a Drive Around

Driving around is an orthodox way of finding flipping deals. All you need to do is step into your vehicle and drive around your target area. Look out for properties that seem distressed, like those with heaps of mail and newspapers, yards filled with overgrown brush, and boarded windows.

If you find a property like this, take down the address and do some investigations of your own to find the owner or seller. This will help you make an offer, and you may end up with a profitable deal.

Check The Internet for Listings

You can locate numerous lists on the internet that show foreclosures, short sales, and distressed properties. Based on the type of list, they may be grouped by city, zip code, or town. These lists are fantastic locations to check when looking for a great flip deal.

You can access many of these lists without a fee, while others may require payment. It's best to start with a free listing as you may find the deal you are after here. There are also a lot of websites available for you to use, like BankForeclosedListings.com and BankForeclosureSale.com.

The above are some of the great ways to find the best investment deals. However, if you fail to familiarize yourself with the essential formula for a flip, you may end up buying properties that won't offer you any revenue. Worse still, you may end up purchasing an overpriced property.

So what is the flipping formula? The next chapter will help you gain a better understanding.

Chapter 8: What is the Financial Formula for **Flipping Homes?**

When it comes to flipping properties, knowing the numbers is of utmost importance. If you want to make the most profit from a flip, you need to know the formula for flipping houses.

In this chapter, we will take a look at some of the essential formulas you need to learn to be successful in this business.

ARV or After Repair Value Formula

The ARV is an approximation of the future value of a home or property after repairs have taken place. It is a property's value after you have made your upgrades.

Numerous factors can affect how you calculate your ARV. The two core areas, though, are the purchase price of the property and the value of repairs.

The formula for calculating ARV is: (Renovation Cost) + (Property Purchase Price)

70% Rule Formula

If you are experienced in flipping homes, you have

probably come across the formula known as the 70 percent rule. You take a home's after repair value and multiply it by 70 percent. Then you deduct the repair cost, and the remainder is what you need to purchase a property if you want to make a significant profit.

The formula for this rule is: (ARV x 70%) – Repair Cost.

When Can You Go Against The 70% Rule?

If you are not an expert at flipping, it is not advisable to go against this rule. However, if you are in a market that is highly competitive and you need to offer higher than 70% to clinch the deal, then do so. There are costly cities like Los Angeles with intense competition, where you may be unable to win a bid at 70% without rehab. In areas like this, you might need to adjust your numbers.

Maximum Buying Price

You need this formula to do an in-depth analysis of the total costs in the project after you have used the 70 percent rule to determine how valuable a property is.

To calculate this, use the formula: ARV - Costs of Repair - Funding Costs - Selling Costs.

Expected Return on Investment

This is the value you anticipate to make once a home has been sold. The higher your ROI (return on investment), the higher your profit. This is what all investors strive for. If your ROI is low, your profit will be too. Your budget, ARV, and timelines will affect your ROI.

To determine the expected ROI, use this formula: Net Profit/Total Investment x 100.

The Formula for Offer Price

The offer price is the amount you are willing to pay on a home. Here, you need to be careful, so you don't pay too much for a property. You want to drop an offer price that is beneficial to you and not too low for the seller.

To determine the offer price, use this formula:

ARV - (Renovation Cost + Holding and Closing Costs + Cost of Financing + Profit Target) = Offer price.

After learning the flipping formula and making the calculations for your next flip, now is the time to make an offer on a home.

Chapter 9: How to Make Offers

Placing an offer to buy a home is a major step, and it can be very unnerving, particularly as it's probably going to be a transaction that requires a lot of cash. You need to ensure the process is as smooth as it can be.

Here, we will take a look at a few tips to help you go through the course of submitting an offer and engaging in negotiations to ensure you have a more seamless transaction.

Crafting a Good Offer

When making an offer on a home, you don't want to make just any offer. It has to be a good offer if you're going to stand a chance of winning the bid. Here are a few essential tips to note when making an offer.

Run a Comparative Market Analysis (CMA)

Before you turn in an offer, request that your real estate agent run a CMA for you. It offers you a current image of your local market, which is vital if the property has been on the market for a while. It also points out a property that is priced beyond its value. For instance, if the CMA proposes a market value in the range of $150,000 - $180,000, and the home is valued at $210,000, you will have the opportunity to negotiate. Your CMA can also offer you a realistic point to begin your initial offer.

Consider Market Indicators

Outside the outcome of a CMA, how long a property has been on the market is an excellent sign of buyer interest. You can find this date in the MLS and other websites for listing homes. Knowing the average time homes in your area spend on the market will provide you with an understanding of the general state of the housing market in that area. It will tell you if it is a seller's market, buyer's market, or none. In the seller's market, homes sell quicker, while in the buyer's market, homes stay on the market longer.

Any offer you make has to show the present local demand and should align with the other offers that may be provided to the seller. For example, a seller whose property has stayed on the market for a long time and battled to draw in bids would be keen on accepting a lower offer as opposed to one who just listed the home. In hot markets, properties may remain on the market for a few hours or days and draw in bids at the list price or above it.

Sill, every situation differs. For example, even in the most competitive seller's market, newer homes that are overpriced and older properties with severe issues battle still can draw in decent offers. When you are uncertain, ask your real estate agent for direction. The same applies if *you* are representing your interests – ask someone who understands the local market for guidance. Even if you know the temperature of the market, you may not have an edge if you don't find out the seller's motivation.

Determine The Motivation of the Seller

The reason behind a seller letting go of his property is just as important to know as the overall temperature of the market. Some sellers need to dispose of their properties fast as we have covered earlier. This may be as a result of financial constraint, relocation, or an urgent desire to amass capital to buy another property. These sellers are called motivated sellers and will often be eager to accept much lower than their asking price, mainly in the buyer's market.

On the other hand, there are sellers who are not in a hurry to sell a property, such as those who inherited a property they don't need. These sellers have no problem waiting for the relevant offers. Watch out for signals, based on what the seller says, to determine the group your seller falls into. In addition to this, it can also be helpful to learn about competing offers.

Learn About Other Offers on the Home

In a lot of jurisdictions, it is not mandatory for sellers to reveal the purchase offers they are considering. It only goes into public record when the seller agrees to an offer. But if you have an experienced real estate agent on your team, they may be able to learn about the other offers you are contending with. Before you tender your offer, ask your agent to find out about showing activity that took place recently from the seller's agent. The agent of the seller may not tell your agent if the seller is considering another offer but may admit if there has been a lot of interest in the property. If you are representing yourself, the responsibility of doing this falls on you.

If you have a hunch that the seller has various offers available, waste no time in submitting your offer, and ensuring the offer is as seller-friendly as it can be. This means a higher offer price and fewer costs paid by the seller. If you suspect that the seller does not have many offers on the property, submit a more buyer-friendly offer, as you will probably have the chance to negotiate.

Get a Pre-Approval Letter if it Is a Financed Deal

If you are getting financing, request that your lender provides you with a letter of pre-approval. This letter will show that you have provisional approval for a mortgage loan up to a specific amount. To get this letter, you may have to schedule a meeting with a loan officer, agree to a credit check, and make asset and income verification information available.

This is different from a final loan approval, as pre-approval enhances the certainty that your application for a loan will eventually be approved. Because of the slim possibility of final approval, lots of sellers don't take financed offers seriously if there are no pre-approval documents attached to it. If the transaction is in cash, pre-approval is not needed as it does not involve any financing.

Make A Larger Down Payment

The more cash that comes with your offer, the more appealing it will look to the seller. The reason for this is that smaller loans have a lower possibility of failure due to an issue with financing.

Get an Attorney to Analyze the Offer

Purchase offers for real estate are one of the vital legal documents you will need to sign. Even if it is not required by the laws of your state that a licensed attorney be present to create purchase offers, it can be a massive benefit to you to get an attorney to analyze your offer and make sure you are not walking into a trap.

Engaging in Negotiations

Before you go into the process of negotiation or sealed bidding, you need to determine the amount you want to spend and think critically before you go beyond that amount. You need to remember that there are extra costs that come with purchasing a property.

Best Bidding Strategies

The best bidding tactic is dependent on the process of bidding – if they are the typical open negotiations or sealed bids. We will be taking a look into each below:

Open negotiations

Start your bid low

Similar to any other form of negotiation, you need to begin low. A good idea would be to make your offer 5 – 10 percent less than the seller's asking price. Remember that many sellers consider this and list their homes for higher than they would accept or anticipate.

Typically, the agent will inform you of any bids that are higher than yours and offer you the opportunity for a second or sometimes third bid. You should only make an offer higher than the asking price if you are aware the seller has already gotten a similar offer, and you believe there are numerous other buyers.

Stay Calm

Remain calm and polite always. If you get frustrated, you will only push people off.

Play Hard to Get

Play hard to get; however, remember to be realistic. If you believe you are dealing with a desperate seller, it may not suit you to seem too interested.

Reach Out to Sellers Directly

It may be helpful to directly reach out to the seller and make your negotiations in person. But note that they could be more challenging to negotiate with as opposed to the agent whose aim is to close the deal fast.

Lastly, don't let the other things that come with the deal be your primary motivators. For instance, used white appliances, except when very new, are not usually worth much, and it is easier to convey them with the home than move them.

Sealed Bids

If you are making a bid through sealed bids, you will need to put down your offer in an envelope and literally seal it. Then, the agent will offer all the bids to the seller, who will typically accept the highest. The aim of this is to get the highest price, because buyers who are worried about someone outbidding them, will put in their best offers. Most times, the seller gets higher than their asking price in a sealed bid.

In some locations that have extremely high demands, sealed bids have become the standard. It can be tedious to dig through sealed bids. Although it may be very enticing to offer an amount way beyond your set budget to win the bid, it is essential you keep to your budget.

If in the end, if you bid higher than the asking price, you may not be covered by your mortgage company. So you need to ensure you have the financing required before you make a bid.

Holding Deposits

Some sellers demand that a buyer provides a little bit of money alongside their offer. It is known as a holding deposit. It is to prove that they see the offer as important enough to invest their money.

Not every seller requests a holding deposit. The ones who request for it are in very hot markets.

There are numerous kinds of holding deposits such as:

- Refundable deposits irrespective of the

party that backs out

- Non-refundable deposits if you, the buyer, walks away. However, there will not be a refund if the buyer walks away. This gets rid of buyers who have no plans of buying the property.

- Non-refundable deposits. These should be avoided because it implies that the seller can sell to another individual and you will only be able to get your cash back if you take them to court.

Holding deposits are not encouraged by many real estate agents. There are a few who don't support them at all because they make the deal take pointlessly longer. Lastly, never offer a holding deposit to the seller directly. The solicitor of the seller usually places the deposit into an escrow account. After submitting your bids, you need to be ready for the possible counteroffers from sellers.

Seller Counteroffers and Responses

The moment you turn in your purchase offer, the seller will need to respond when the consideration window ends. If the seller has a lot of offers on the property, and your offer is not one of the most appealing, the seller may disregard the offer.

The most common ways sellers respond to purchase offers are by:

Agreeing to The Terms

When the seller is fine with the offer, they accept it and signs a written agreement, which then establishes a binding purchase agreement. Making adjustments is still possible up until the closing date, so long as both parties are in agreement and have signed a contract.

Rejecting/Refusing The Terms

If the terms of the offer do not favor the seller, the seller can reject the offer. Although dealing with rejection is painful, the significant part is that the seller is willing to interact with you. This means you can follow up on the rejection with an offer that is more seller-friendly.

Make a Counteroffer

When the offer is appealing, but not wholly satisfactory, the seller can alter it by making changes to core aspects like the price of purchase and seller-paid expenses. Then they sign it and send it back to you, the buyer. This is called a counteroffer. You can decide to agree with the counteroffer in writing, or further alter it, sign it and send it to the seller once more to analyze. This process can last for as long as needed until the seller agrees with the offer or one party stops negotiations.

In a few situations, sellers who get many offers at the same time, individually negotiate with every buyer to get the best deal they can. If the seller needs to reach a binding agreement quickly, they may request that each buyer who has an interest provides their best offer possible, and go with the best one.

After you make an offer on a property, the next step will be to do your due diligence before you finally close the deal.

Chapter 10: Doing Your Due Diligence

Due diligence is the act of conducting research before you buy a property. The kind of home you want to buy is not vital, but if you're going to reduce all of the risks, then you need to do a few things. Ensure you do an inspection of the property and an appraisal, as those are some things you require for due diligence.

It does not have to stop here. If you are purchasing a property, you can do an investigation of your own. In this chapter, we will be covering all that has to do with due diligence. It also consists of due diligence tips, which will ensure any house flipping transaction is a success.

The Legal Due Diligence

It is not possible to determine everything about a property at a glance. For this reason, you have to consider the title, deeds, and zoning, and other factors.

Due Diligence Tasks

Due diligence aims to find out whether all your projections in the initial analysis of the project are correct or wrong. In essence, you will be using this time to make sure you have all the needed numbers to go forward with the project or not.

If you have gotten to this point, you should already be through with the majority of your due diligence tasks. However, it may not be as comprehensive as you need it to be. With this knowledge, here are a few things to do when finishing the purchase:

Do Your Homework

Take a walk around the property. Check out any documents before you sign, calculate the cost of insurance and other expenses, take a look at trends in the environment and other market values.

You need to do all you can to make sure the property you are buying will bring in good returns. Be detailed as you weigh the benefits and drawbacks of your prospective investment. When it comes to due diligence, there is no detail too minute.

Be prepared for an appraisal, if financing. An appraisal defines the property's value. If you have plans to take out a mortgage, lenders will need you to perform an appraisal to make sure the property is worth its value. After an assessment, if the property is not worth its value, you will not get an approval for the loan except if the seller reduces the cost to what the property is determined to be worth.

A home inspector and an appraiser will help in inspecting the property. However, the appraiser deliberates on things like location, size of property, upgrades, and other conditions. Then the appraiser will compare it to other properties in the area similar to what you want to buy in the area. When you do an appraisal, sellers will be unable to increase the prices without value.

Go Through the Title History

Carrying out a title search before you go on with the final purchase process of a property is vital to ensure you will get the title clear and free of any ownership issues. If the past owner has previously done some work on the property and has failed to make complete payment of the full amount to the contractor, the property may come with a lien attached that needs to be paid before they can sell the property. If the buyer has no information about this lien, it could lead to them paying for the pending amount before they can release the title clear and free in your name.

After carrying out a title search, it is essential that you get owner's title insurance to save you from challenges that may not have been revealed when searching the title. These kinds of problems can include:

- Forgery

- Undisclosed heirs

- Deeds omissions

- Recording mistakes etc.

The owner's title insurance safeguards you from unidentified liens on the property that may come up after you close. Insurance companies have a responsibility to clear these up.

Take a Look at Homeowners Association Restrictions and Covenants

If you are purchasing an apartment, condo, single-family home, or townhouse in specific areas, be prepared to follow HOA requirements. HOAs often come with strict covenants and regulations that owners must adhere to. These contracts are put in place and enforced to safeguard the neighborhood's values and appearance.

For example, there may be a limitation or restriction to the color you can paint the exterior of your property. The same could also apply to parking an RV on the street or driveway. If you go against any of these rules, you may be liable to pay fines to the HOA. You need to go through the restrictions and covenants of the HOA before you purchase any property.

Inspect The Property

You need to inspect your property. The inspection will be one of your final chances to ensure you are purchasing a sound property.

You will want to hire a licensed home inspector to help with the inspection instead of doing it on your own. However, you need to note that home inspectors are not perfect and can miss issues. Home inspectors only take note of things that you have to replace or repair. This information is significant, but it is not *all* the data you need to make a calculated decision. Here are some other areas you will want to cover:

- Find out if the property has a lot of radon. It is known to cause cancer.

- Ensure there is no mold in the home.

- If there is a well instead of public water, you need to check the water quantity and quality.

- If the house was developed before 1978, you might want to find out if there is lead paint. This is vital if you have kids below the age of six.

Preparing for The Inspection of a Property

It is necessary for you to get ready for the inspection of the property by noting down parts of the home you want the inspector to check before they show up. Your checklist should consist of:

- Foundation

- Exterior paint

- Appliances

- Driveways and walkways

- Attic space

- Roof

- Downspouts and rain gutters

- Power outlets, electrical panel, and light switches

- Floors, ceilings, and walls

- Windows and doors

- HVAC system, heating, cooling and thermostats

- Water heater, plumbing fixtures, and faucets

- Garage

- Basement

- Balconies and Porches

- Railings, steps, and stairs

A proper inspection should last for a few hours. Ensure you are physically present so you can learn as much as you can about the condition of the property. Put down notes of your own, take pictures, and ask questions.

What a Home Inspection May Not Entail

Although an inspection scope may differ, the primary concern of inspectors are the physical aspects of the home. This may cover a lot of things, but it may not cover everything. Some things that may be ignored which you will need to check out yourself include:

- Landscaping and trees

- Sewer lines

- Lawn sprinklers

- Odors

- Drainage

- Internet and cell service

- Chimney and fireplace

- Swimming pool equipment

- Rats, mice, and other rodents

- Wood-destroying pests like carpenter ants and termites

- Floors hidden by carpeting

There are numerous kinds of inspections you need to perform on a property you want to invest in. We will be taking a look at some of the types of checks you can carry out and why it would be beneficial to spend some of your funds to get specific inspections done before you make a purchase.

Note that it is beneficial to be physically present during the inspection, as this will help you better understand the property's condition and offers the chance to ask any questions that may come up.

General Home Inspection

Before you go ahead with the purchase process of a home, you need to perform a general inspection. The majority of lenders require this inspection if you are getting a loan. Typically, a licensed contractor or home inspector with the right certifications will examine everything in the home. This consists of a complete report on the situation of cooling, roof, electrical, water heater, kitchen appliances, and heating. The inspector will offer you an elaborate report on any problems they find and how serious those problems may be.

After the general inspection, it is not unusual to find out that there are necessary repairs you need to do, which might bring about possible expenses and dangers. There are times when the costs for these essential repairs will be high enough to result in the buyer canceling an offer and continue their search for a property with less risk. Ensure the language in your purchase agreement includes conditions that let you cancel your offer after an inspection. It should also protect you from losing any cash you have put in as a down payment.

(WDO) Wood-Destroying Organisms Inspection

Many lenders also ask you to do a WDO inspection of a property. This inspection allows you to determine if there is any wood rot in a property's structure. Water damage or termites can lead to wood rot and inspectors will check the interior walls, garage and exterior sliding for this kind of damage.

Deep wood rot can depreciate the structural integrity of a property. In the report presented to you, the inspector will let you know the severity of the wood rot or how minor it is. This will provide you with extra information to aid you in determining if the risks are more than the returns.

Lead-Based Paint Inspection

This is an inspection required by law for homes developed earlier than 1978. If the seller knows that there is a presence of lead-based paint in the exterior or interior of the house, they are legally bonded to convey this information to prospective buyers.

You, as the buyer, also need to carry out your tests own for lead-based paint as part of your due diligence. This form of paint is dangerous to the health and will cost money to get rid of before you or anyone else can live in the property.

Radon Gas Inspection

Inspection for radon gas is not as common as the other aforementioned inspection types. However, this gas can be found in houses all around the United States. The Surgeon General and EPA also states that being exposed to this gas for long periods has been proven to contribute to numerous deaths related to lung cancer each year.

Once the inspections are complete, you will be left

with the following options:

- Going ahead with the sale after accepting the condition

- Walking away from the deal

- Renegotiating for a more suitable deal

If everything seems sound, go ahead and sign a document that informs the seller that you agree with the conditions.

However, if there are serious problems with the property, what do you do? In a situation like this, you can first renegotiate the deal before you walk away. For instance, if you notice faulty plumbing and there needs to be a complete change in the plumbing, don't take off yet; you can request that the seller carries out the repairs or deducts the fixing cost from the sale's value.

Run Your Numbers Once More

This is the final step in your due diligence. Using all of the data you have gathered above, now you need to run the numbers once more with the more elaborate data that you have obtained. Generating the information, you need to decide for the last time what the core objective of the process of due diligence is. It will help you determine if you should move on with the deal or not.

Here, you need to use the data available at your disposal to find out if the property will generate an acceptable revenue if you buy, rehab, and resell. If the potential for profit is acceptable to you, then you can move on with the deal. However, if it isn't, you need to check out other options.

Steps to Take if the Numbers Are Not Right

Hopefully, this won't be the case. However, there are times when you will notice that the numbers you come up with during the process of due diligence will show that the deal is not as good as it seemed at the agreed-upon price.

The way you deal with this situation has a huge role to play on if you plan to continuously make returns from flipping homes or make a profit only a few times. In some cases, house flippers get attached to deals and go ahead with them even when the numbers are not right. During these kinds of situations, all they are doing is postponing the challenges that arise with going through with a bad deal.

So, if you find out after your due diligence that the numbers are not right, what options are available to you? Check them out below:

Request for a Reduction in Price

Heading back to the seller and asking for a reduction in price is your initial course of action. Most times, being honest can make things go smoother. Reach out to the seller and inform them that your numbers are not right, and request they offer you support for your findings.

For instance, if you observed a list of hidden issues that require repairs during the process of due diligence, you can provide the seller with a list. In many situations, if you can prove to the seller that your new information during the process of due diligence that has an impact on the deal, they will be eager to consider reducing the price. If it is an REO deal, the bank will often need contractor bids or inspection reports before they will deliberate on a reduction of rates based on issues that came up during the process of due diligence.

Walk Away from The Deal

If you are unable to get a reduced price on the deal, you may have to walk away from the agreement. Your agent, contractors, and sellers may be unhappy, but this would be much better than investing in a property that would bring you no revenue.

If your due diligence comes out with great results, then you can go ahead with the project. If you do your due diligence the right way and hire the wrong contractor, you may still end up dealing with losses. The next chapter outlines the steps involved in hiring contractors.

Chapter 11: Hiring Contractors

You have put most of what you need in place, and now it is time for you to build another vital team: the team of contractors who will have the responsibility of getting you a decent profit for your investment. Great contractors are those who will transform your property from inhabitable to ready to sell.

However, you need to understand that finding a team of contractors with skills you can rely on is one of the most complex aspects of this business. The truth is, the number of great contractors is much lower than the unreliable ones. This is something that is not inevitable in the industry. Anyone can name himself as a contractor after buying a bunch of tools, and that makes the field saturated with numerous unskilled contractors.

How can you ensure you don't fall into the hands of unscrupulous workers and ensure you don't drown in unnecessary delays and hassles? This is what we will be covering in this chapter. Before going any further, you need to determine the kind of contractor you require for your project.

What Type of Contractor Do You Need?

Depending on the kind of project you want to work on, the following are contractors you may have to hire:

- General Contractor: This is one who oversees all areas of a project, like obtaining building permits, hiring and managing subcontractors, and setting appointments for inspections.

- Architect: An individual who deals with core renovations and designs homes. They are especially handy when your project involves alterations to the structure of a home.

- Specialty Contractor: These help in the installation of specific products like bathroom fixtures, and kitchen cabinets, among others.

- Build/Design Contractor: A contractor who offers both building and design services.

The majority of the time, your best bet will be to go with a general contractor as many of them can cover all other aspects of a project. Let's take a look at how you can find the right contractor for your project.

Finding the Right Contractor for Your Project

Hiring a general contractor can be of immense benefit to you. They are professionals in the field and can make constructive decisions on your behalf. For instance, if you want to make changes to a particular part of the home, your contractor would let you know whether it would lead to damage to the property or if it's a solid idea.

The general contractor largely supervises the project from the beginning to end without wasting any time, because their major role is to ensure the project goes smoothly. As opposed to doing it yourself, where you often make efforts to correct mistakes numerous times before you get it right, getting the services of a general contractor ensures the project goes right the first time.

Another benefit of hiring a general contractor is their capacity to help you develop a financial plan, which can keep the project going until it is over. They can let you know the cost of material and how much you will need to pay laborers. They will also let you know the timescales of a project, all of which are only possible because of the vast field of experience they have.

As a professional, a contractor is knowledgeable of

the permits you need in various kinds of property renovations. This will ensure you don't get into legal trouble, as if you fail to obtain a necessary permit, you will be held liable and not the contractor. A contractor can also determine the aspects of the jobs they can take part in even if there is no available permit. With this, your project will always be ongoing and drawing closer to completion.

Places to Find Your Contractor

If you are in search of a contractor, here are some resources to consider:

Referrals from Real Estate Investment Clubs (REIC)

Contractors are always on the move or getting some work done. They do not remain in a location holding for people to hire them. One of the best places to begin is your reliable local REIC. The investors who are present in these meetings will likely be able to refer you to a decent contractor. And since you can be confident they have collaborated with them beforehand, you can rest assured that the contractors will have an excellent track record. The kinds of connections you make here can prove to be of immense benefit to you.

Ask Subcontractors

Next, if you know other fantastic sub-contractors, you can ask which general contractors they have collaborated with previously who they can endorse. Skilled subcontractors love partnering with great general contractors, so they usually have an idea of which contractors are efficient and which are not.

Check Out Your Farm Area

Taking a drive or walk around your farm area to look for contractors doing some work close-by is another means of finding contractors. Pull over or stop and begin a conversation. It offers you an opportunity to see how they carry out their projects and the kind of services they render in real-life scenarios.

Check Hardware Stores

You can locate general contractors at a Home Depot or other home improvement store. They are easy to spot once you are inside because they would be the ones purchasing a reasonable amount of supplies for rehabbing homes. The same as before, approach them and strike up a conversation.

Check Online

If you want something straightforward, the internet

remains your best bet. Sometimes, all you need to do is run a search online for local contractors to find one close to you. To take it a step further, search Craigslist ads or ads on similar platforms where you can find contractors close to you. The only downside of this method is that you may find a lot of unskilled talent and may need to do a lot of work in choosing the most reliable worker. If you don't have many other options, though, this is a great way to begin.

Get a feel of them over the phone and go with your gut. Request references which you will be able to reach out to and ask them to show you the projects they have finished. Once you are through with the initial stage of finding a group of contractors you think would be great for the job, you will need to further narrow your options to the best candidates by asking them a few questions.

Questions to Ask Before You Hire a Contractor

It usually is less challenging to locate an individual that has worked for another investor previously. These individuals will understand that with you, they have the benefit of repeat work. By working with you, there is a possibility that they may not need to continually compete for jobs.

That being said, with this knowledge, the following

are questions you need to ask a contractor before you hire:

Have You Worked for Someone Similar?

First, you need to ask if they have previously worked for someone in the house flipping business. If their response is yes, ask the number of jobs they have completed and the type of work done on those projects.

How Long Have You Been in This Job?

You need to find out how long the contractor has been in the field. As judgmental as it may seem, what you want is someone who has had ample experience in the field. This would mean they would be able to deal with any problem that arises. They will also have an understanding of the permits you need to make sure you don't fall into legal hitches.

Do You Work Alone?

You need to find out if they work without extra hands. There are benefits and drawbacks to this. A contractor who has helpers would be more expensive, but work progress would be faster. One without helpers may not cost as much, but work progress might be slowed. They are both good options, so long as you have weighed the benefits and drawbacks.

Supposing they do work with people, ask how many people they have on their team. If they have a small team, the contractor would not be an ideal option for a huge rehab project.

Is There Any Area You Don't Work On?

Ask if there is a specific part of the job they don't do. Can they work on plumbing and electrical? How about framing and roofing? You need to determine beforehand if there are areas they are uncomfortable working on. You don't want to incur additional expenses by hiring a contractor who does not do specific jobs and end up hiring someone else to fill in those blanks. It's best to go with someone versatile who can handle all aspects of a given project.

Are You Presently Working On Any Project?

This is an essential question to work. Rehab takes time, and the quicker you close, the faster you get your returns. If the contractor is busy with other projects, find out when they will be through. You don't want your project to be on hold for a few months, pending when a contractor will be free. What you need is someone who can begin as soon as possible.

Do You Have the Required License?

A license is vital and shows the level of skill and

dedication a contractor has to their profession. However, in some areas, you can overlook this. If you are not doing an extensive rehab, a license may not be essential. Some contractors don't have a license but will have associates they can get these from if the need arises. However, if you want to be on the safe side, it is best to go with a licensed contractor.

Do You Have Insurance?

This is another very significant question. You need to find out if your contractor is insured. In the event of an injury, while working on your property, hospital bills can consume a whole lot of funds you could have used for other things. The same is also applicable in case there is damage to your property while working.

There are a few essential insurance coverages a contractor should have which include:

- Personal liability

- Property damage coverage

- Worker's compensation

Do not forget to request copies of current insurance certificates. With the right insurance you are indemnified from all the charges that may arise during the process of working on your project. There are a few things you may not find out from asking questions, and you can determine these by watching out for a few signs.

Signs to Look Out for When Choosing a Contractor

- If a contractor offers you a price much lower than it should be or less than other bids, you need to be careful. Sometimes, cheaper is not better. Many times, contractors who have not been working for a while will require your job to pay their pending bills, individuals they owe or just to complete past projects they have already begun. This is a regular occurrence, and you need to exercise caution.

- Other times, shady contractors will inform you that they don't have sufficient funds to finish your job and require another deposit. The challenge with this could be that you have already settled them for your job, but the funds were channeled somewhere else. They will go down a slope and pull you in with them.

- Watch out for contractors who will try to appeal to your emotions by telling you a sad story in a bid to give them the job. It is okay to feel bad for them, but keep in mind that you are running a business and if your gut screams

NO! you need to move on to the next candidate.

- Stay away from the ones who appear to have substance abuse problems. If you come across a contractor who smells like a brewery or has erratic behavior indicative of drug use, you will want to move on to your next option. When picking a contractor you need someone in the right frame of mind, as errors can be very costly during a rehab project.

- Hiring a contractor without insurance is a horrible idea. The moment you find out they have no insurance, move on to the next candidate.

- Next, you need to stay away from contractors who request half the payment in advance. Many rehabbers have fallen into this trap and are left with a contractor who refuses to show up until you make numerous calls to them. Other times, they never even show up at all, and it would be a hassle to get your money back. Note that this method may work for some people, but if you are working with a contractor for the first time, it might be a good idea to avoid this scenario.

- Lastly, stay away from the ones who

brag a lot. This may seem awkward, but in numerous cases, those who have a constant need to remind you of how great they are at their jobs are often anything but. Sometimes, contractors brag to prep you for the huge bid they are about to make. If you come across one who boasts a lot, move on to someone else.

Get Numerous Bids

Hold on for the bids to come falling in and try your best not to involve yourself in games. Some contractors will want to draw out information to determine what the others are bidding or tell you to state your price. Do all you can to avoid this and request that they all provide their bids. It is vital for you to have a scope of work in place, showing in detail the job you want to do to make things easier.

Speak to the candidates left and decide on the one you prefer the most after considering all the costs. If you made it evident to them that you would be offering lots of work opportunities, the bid they provided should be well within their comfort zone and yours. Even if you are okay with the price, try to engage in a little negotiation with every one of them and see what happens. As a rule of thumb, always ensure you negotiate even if you can only cut down the bid a little. You don't want the contractor feeling like they could have gotten much more.

Analyze the Job

Once you have chosen your contractor and they have begun to work on the project, you need to watch them closely. Watch how he works and note anything you are not okay with. Some people act their best when bidding for a job, but the instant they get it, they begin to do the opposite of what they offered. This is why it is very crucial to watch closely. If you are not satisfied with the way a contractor works, what can you do?

What to Do About an Unreliable Contractor

If your chosen contractor fails to meet his end of the bargain in an agreement, you are within your rights to terminate the contract. You don't have to keep up with issues to prevent confrontation. Some contractors are experienced at testing boundaries and would push you to your limits. And once they observe that you won't confront them, they will keep doing as they please knowing they can get away with it.

When things are not going as they should, you need to set things right. Do not keep enduring in the hopes that things will get better, because the truth is that it hardly ever does. Request corrections if something is not going the way it should. This may be difficult, but it is an essential step you need to take once you notice any problems.

Understand Your Options of Payment

When working with contractors, you need to understand the payment options available to you. These tips can help:

- Avoid paying in cash: For projects that are not too big, you can pay via credit card or check. Lots of individuals make arrangements for financing to pay for more significant projects.

- Place a limit on down payment: There are laws in specific states that restrict the amount of cash a contractor can ask for as a down payment. Reach out to your local or state consumer agency to learn about the laws in your region.

- Make efforts to provide payments in milestones upon completion of clearly stated amounts of work. In doing this, if the work is not progressing as it should, contractors would not get payments on time as well. One more thing which is as important as understanding your payment options is your contract.

Draw Up a Written Contract

Different states have varying contract requirements. Even if it is not essential to draw up a written agreement in your place of residence, you need to request one. It should be concise, clear, detailed, and should consist of all the project essentials. Before signing any contract, make sure it includes the following:

- The name, phone number, license number, and address of the contractor

- A projected start and finish date

- The schedule of payment for the contractor, suppliers, and subcontractors

- The obligation of the contractor to get all the permits required

- How the contractor will deal with change orders. A change order is an authorization to the contractor, put down in writing, for them to make changes alongside the work defined in the main contract, and could have an impact on the project's schedule and cost.

- Information regarding warranties that cover workmanship and materials, as well as the addresses and names of the individuals who will honor them; in this case, this could include the manufacturer, contractors, and distributors. The warranty length and other restrictions should be clearly stated.

- The roles of the contractor and things they are not obligated to do. For instance, is cleaning up the site a part of the price? Request for a broom clause, which holds the contractor liable for all tasks related to cleaning, including stains and spills.

- An elaborate outline of all the materials, including every product's size, model, cost, and brand. If there are materials to be selected later on, the contract should indicate the individual charged with picking each item and the amount of money allocated to it.

- A statement of your right to revoke the contract within three working days, if the contract was signed in your residence or any location that is not the permanent site of business of the seller.

After Hiring a Contractor

Hiring the contractor is only the first step. After hiring, there are a few things to do to ensure your collaboration runs smoothly.

Keep detailed records

Ensure all the paperwork that has to do with your project is in one location. The paperwork may include:

- Change orders

- Copies of contract

- History of every payment (you may require receipts for tax purposes).

- All communications with your home improvement professionals

You may also want to keep a journal or record of all of your discussions, actions, and phone calls. You may also need to take pictures as progress is made on the project. These records are essential, especially if issues arise with your job during the construction process or after.

Release Payments Wisely

Do not complete the final payment until you are pleased with the work. In addition to being pleased with the tasks completed, it is vital to find out if suppliers and subcontractors have been settled, as well. Your state laws may give them the capacity to file a mechanic's lien against your property to fulfill any pending bills, compelling you to let go of your home to get them made whole. Look out for yourself by requesting the contractor, and all suppliers and subcontractors, sign a lien waiver or lien release.

Be Aware of the Limit for the Final Bill

There are local or state laws that restrict the amount the final fee can go beyond the estimate unless the increase has been approved by you. Look into these laws so you can be prepared.

Know When You Can Deny Payment

If you have issues with the services or items charged to a credit card, and you have tried to sort things out with the seller, you are within your rights to reach out to the company operating your credit card to deny payment for the services or items. You will be able to withhold payment up to the remaining amount of credit for the purchase, alongside any finance or associated charges.

Take Advantage of a Sign-Off Checklist

Before making the final payment, ensure that the following conditions have been met:

- All tasks are in accordance with the standards stated in the contract

- You have warranties in writing for

workmanship and materials

- You have evidence that payment has been made to suppliers and subcontractors

- The work site has been cleared and cleaned up of surplus materials, equipment, and tools

- You have reviewed and accepted the work done

After getting your team of contractors in place, and work has kicked off on your property, you need to learn proper management to ensure everything goes as it should. Move on to the next chapter to learn how to do this efficiently.

Chapter 12: Managing Your Rehab

If you have gotten this far, it means you have most of what you need in place. However, even if you got the services of an excellent contractor, you may still need to manage the project to ensure everything goes as it should. When it comes to projects, the art of efficient project management is essential.

Any delay in the completion of a project, even as little as a day, means extra costs for you. So your goal should be to ensure you complete a project as quickly as possible without compromising quality. If you have a lot of people working for you, it is another compelling reason to complete projects fast. Presuming you have a team of 3 working on your project, whom you pay $20 per hour, that could add up to $400 daily. This means, for each day your project, you spend an additional $400, not including any other expenses. This makes it vital to complete projects as fast as prudently possible.

To ensure the project goes as it should, you need to have your scope of work in place and create a project schedule. Don't wait until you have closed a deal before putting these together. You need to have an idea of what you plan on doing and the costs it will entail before you sign any contract. As we covered earlier, the moment you have the property under contract, you need to do your due diligence and make sure you have a thorough understanding of all you need to do.

With that in mind, how do you make sure you manage your project effectively? Here are the things you need to put in place and do.

Make a detailed plan

Before you do any work, ensure you have already finalized your design. Instead of designing on the go, the rehab process is smoother when you don't have to make continuous changes. If you have no plan in place, you may see that available options are limited depending on the work that has been done already.

Weeks before the project, take some time to draw up plans, outline your specifications, and ensure you have made every decision before you move on. This will help you save money and time as you go on, and would drastically minimize the level of frustration for everyone involved in the project.

Don't Assume

When putting together a plan, don't assume any other involved party will understand your vision for the project except as it is explicitly stated. Put down every detail, even to the most seemingly irrelevant one. It is better to seem fussy than to be left with preventable mistakes that lead to disputes later on in the project.

For instance, if the bathroom will not be appealing if you use a specific color, ensure you state the color you want. If you don't specify what you want, you can't expect to see it come to fruition during the project. To avoid this, list *everything*.

Prepare the Scope of Work

Some general contractors will manage all aspects of a project. However, many of them don't do things like plumbing or electrical. Also, if you are hiring subcontractors or other service providers, you will need to have a clear outline of the work they need to do and the work they can't do, which you will allocate to other vendors. So after creating a list of all the work that your project entails, you will have to determine who you are going to assign the tasks to. A typical way of doing this is as follows:

- Check out the utilities

- Demolition

- Structural repairs, if needed

- Flooring

- Painting

- General construction, which may include interior and exterior

- Appliances and other facilities

- Checking of systems

- Cleaning

This is a flexible one, which means you can shuffle things up as you see fit. For instance, if the weather is great, and the HVAC vendor is occupied for the next two days or more, you don't need to stop work, because your employees and contractors won't have any issues with the weather conditions while working on your property. Also, you can do two things on the list at the same time. Work in the interior can begin the same time you are trimming the trees. The key thing here is to have a plan in place showing who is going to do each task and listing all the vendors before you begin anything.

Make Sure You Are All in Agreement

The next step, after creating the scope of work is to ensure you are all on the same page. You need to provide a detailed copy of your specifications to each of the vendors and subcontractors. Talk to them about the specifications and see areas they may be able to offer better suggestions.

When they know beforehand what part of the property an additional toilet or bathroom would be located, for example, the builders will know to leave a bit of space for pipes and other plumbing materials before plastering everything. This prevents the extra mess of breaking down walls to allocate pipes.

Dealing with Service Providers

Sadly, many vendors tend to disappoint. If you are collaborating with a vendor who flakes on appointments and can't be relied on to meet a specific schedule, you may have to schedule someone else. Knowing this, try not to ask contractors for a particular date a project will be completed. Unexpected things tend to happen, and a project may take more time than anticipated.

Nonetheless, you will want to ensure things are scheduled as close as possible without any complications. If there are occasions where two vendors can do their task simultaneously, don't hesitate to do it. You want to keep them as tightly scheduled as you can. For instance, plan the flooring shortly after construction and so on.

A good idea would be to use project management software or a spreadsheet to create a plan for everything, and monitor the completed tasks, list what needs to be scheduled and what has already been scheduled. This is vital because forgetting to do something minor during the construction stage may cause a long delay that could have been avoided from the start.

Do Not Alter Your Decisions

During a rehab, your contractor or builder may have many questions as work is ongoing. Some questions you may have to address include:

- Where should I put these lights?

- What color should be here?

The easiest way to deal with this is to consider as many of these questions as you can beforehand and have a response for them. Better still, let the information be in your specifications. When you are under pressure, you could begin to act on impulse, which might lead to regret later on. Taking too much time, on the other hand, can cause a delay in the project, which will cost you money and time down the road.

It is impossible to avoid questions you did not plan for, but anywhere possible, request that your contractors give you time to decide, without any delay to the project. It is fine to ask for their opinion, but do not choose under pressure.

Have a Contingency in Place

Even after you have planned as best as you should, there may be times when problems that you could not have seen coming, would crop up during your project. It is a great idea to have a plan B in your budget to accommodate issues like these, especially in a building that is quite old. You never can tell what condition you would find the walls when you tear up the kitchen cabinets.

In situations like this, you need to have a contingency in place instead of been thrown off your tracks when issues like these occur. Weigh the options available and make a decision. Your contractors would be able to advise you on the step to take, so take advantage of their experience and find the best course of action.

Don't Pay Contractors for Work Before Completion

Many new rehabbers have fallen into this trap and paid the total sum before the job even began. Most times, they lose their money as the contractor leaves town with the cash and never answers their phone again. Some are lucky and can get their work completed after incessant calls to the contractor, but the damage has already been done as the work takes twice the time it should have.

To prevent this, you need to make payments in milestones. For instance:

- 15% of the money up front to begin

- 1/3 of the balance paid after completing 1/3 of the task

- 1/3 of the balance after completing 2/3 of the job

- Final payment after finishing the work and you are satisfied

Ensure You Are Physically Present

This may not be needed if you are working with a team you trust. However, if you are not going to be present at the property throughout the process, ensure you pay surprise visits every few days.

Many rehabbers make the mistake of telling their contractor the exact time they will be checking in on them. If you are working with a good contractor, this may not be an issue. However, with an unscrupulous contractor, you just armed him with the information he needs to slow down his pace or go do something else during your project time.

Many contractors overbook themselves and will do all they can to complete two jobs simultaneously. This will end up reflecting one or both projects they are dealing with at that moment, all in a bid to make extra cash. You want to make sure that your contractors are not slacking off when you are not present, and they are moving ahead with your task.

Your best bet is to pay surprise visits to your work site without any consistency. If you are unable to go for these surprise checks, you can send in a relative or close friend to help you out with this once in a while as the project is ongoing. This will ensure contractors are always on their toes and channeling all their energy into completing your project.

Know Your Suppliers

There are house flippers who take charge of everything, right down to materials. On the other hand, some rehabbers delegate the tasks to the contractor so they don't have to deal with the stress. The decision lies with you to pick which option you are okay with.

However, you need to understand that contractors will typically choose cheaper materials if you leave it to them. For minor things, this may be fine, but when it has to do with the vital elements in the home like faucets and appliances, you won't want to choose based solely on price.

A better option would be to have a go-to depot

that you have a personal rapport with, and get them to deliver the essential materials at a specific time and leave your contractor to supply the less critical materials.

Hire an Expert

Managing the project on your own can be rewarding, but there are specific skills you need. You need to be confident, strategic, organized, and able to deal with pressure. Also, you need to have time on your hands to supervise the work, which may be impossible if you have other things to do.

If you have the extra cash to invest, you can go the easy way and hire a project manager to do the work for you. It's better to spend more money and get the results you desire than to invest your time and money, battle with stress, and still be left with a poorly done project.

When you are through with the management of your rehab, the ideal result should be a finished project waiting to be sold. The next decision you will have to make after this is to choose between going with an agent or selling FSBO. More on this in the next chapter.

Chapter 13: Agent Versus FSBO

Selling a home is not easy, nor is it rocket science if you know what you are doing. It requires a lot of dedication, time, and hard work, and to save funds, lots of owners do it by themselves. There are benefits and drawbacks to selling a property without the help of a licensed real estate agent, and in the long run, only you can decide the best course of action for your home.

With this in mind, this chapter will be discussing the differences between both options to help you make a choice.

Is it Compulsory to Hire Real Estate Agents?

There is no law binding you to hire a real estate agent when it comes to selling homes. However, agents may be able to access information you won't be able to such as the MLS. If you decide to work with an agent, they will handle a huge chunk of the work ranging from pricing, listing, drawing up paperwork, among others.

FSBO or For Sale by Owner: What Does it Mean?

Sale by owner is when the owner of a property lists it without using a licensed real estate agent. If you decide to take this route, you will handle the entire process of selling the home, from beginning to end.

Agent vs. FSBO: Fees

Many investors who support FSBO choose to sell their properties FSBO because they believe it will save them cash. However, it was observed in a study done by Northwestern University, that of all the properties sold FSBO in Madison, Wisconsin got no less than the same amount of cash as properties sold by licensed agents.

Yes, agents do earn a commission from the sale price of the home, but these fees are channeled to the money and time needed to sell a home. If you decide to sell on your own, you will have to spend money to list the property, host prospective buyers, and stage, all of which require cash.

On the other hand, real estate agents will help take pictures of your home, stage, and list it on the MLS, which can only be accessed by agents. If you collaborate with an agent, you won't need to pay the fees involved in listing a home. Real estate agents will also host property viewings and open houses by themselves, which means you can concentrate on other activities. Also, if you sell FSBO, you will still have to pay some agent's fees.

Marketing

You need the right buyers for a successful home sale. As stated in a study carried out by the National Association of Realtors, 90 percent of individuals who wanted to purchase homes searched online. Real estate agents have the MLS and other methods of getting visibility both online and offline. In contrast, as an FSBO seller, you can buy ads in newspapers or using online social media platforms.

Time

The longer a property stays on the market, the less the potential selling price. It was observed by the National Association of Realtors that properties sold via the MLS, sold 20 days quicker on average, while 20 percent of the listings done FSBO had to re-renewed because they were unable to sell.

There is a lot of time involved in scheduling property viewings, staging, and getting offers on a home. Agents invest a lot of time, sometimes during holidays and often during weekends to ensure that the house sells for the appropriate amount as fast as possible. If you have a full-time job and decide to sell FSBO, you may need to cut down your work hours to do home showings, which means a reduction on your paycheck as well. Even if you don't work full time, are you ready to invest all of your time in showings and marketing? Would you be willing to drop all you are doing to meet up with a prospective buyer when they want to see a home?

If you are unable to do all of these, your home may spend more time on the market, and many buyers see this as a red flag even if you have a good reason for it.

Negotiation

Selling a home is a legal deal. For this reason, you will have to negotiate with buyers. If you turn over this role to a real estate agent, they will deal with negotiations on your behalf. However, as an FSBO seller, you would need to do the negotiations on your own. A real estate agent typically negotiates with the buyer's attorney, agent, the buyer themself, and the bank appraiser. The experience the real estate agent has underneath their belt makes all of these a breeze for them. However, if you sell FSBO, you will need to do the strategizing on your own and depend on your skills and expertise, which may not yet be developed, especially as a new seller.

Even investors with lots of experience stick to using agents. This is because they sell homes for a living, and know the inner workings of selling a home. They understand how the market in your environment works and are professionals when it comes to selling homes. Real estate agents sell two to four homes weekly, which is a record you may not be able to beat anytime soon.

Legal Assistance

The sale of a home is a legitimate deal. If you choose to sell your property on your own, some states would not authorize you to go through the process of closing without the presence of a real estate agent. Also, unless you understand legal documents, you may miss some vital piece of information when signing a contract and be left with a lawsuit later on.

An experienced agent understands all the legal workings of selling a home and can aid in ensuring you don't have to deal with a lawsuit later on.

Which Is the Ideal Option For You?

Selling FSBO should be the last option on your list when you want to sell a home. The benefits offered by a real estate agent outweighs the drawbacks you face when selling FSBO. Nevertheless, the final decision lies with you, and whether you believe you can handle all the risks involved. Only you know the best course of action for your business.

Chapter 14: Staging

If you want the sale of your home to be quicker, staging it lets you show it in its best look, inspiring potential buyers to view themselves residing there. It enables you to stay ahead in a competitive market, as buyers of homes are getting used to seeing staged homes, both in online listings and in person.

Staging A Home: What Does it Mean?

At its core, staging has to do with the enhancement of an item, thereby making it more appealing to buyers, which in turn boosts its value. If you head to a store, you would be more likely to pay more if the product comes in a nice package and it is displayed in a nice way. If it seems to be in poor condition, you may not want to pay as much. The same is applicable when selling a property.

Home staging has to do with preparing your property for the market and marketing its selling points. You do this by creating an emotional and visual appeal which will pull in buyers, to imagine what life in that home would be like. Buying a home is an emotional decision as well as a financial one. The buyer must have the capacity to envision themselves residing in the home, living the lifestyle portrayed by the home, to create the craving to buy that house. You need to understand that even though the property you did your best to fix and flip is an investment to you – *you* need to make buyers feel like the home is the ideal one for *them*.

Does Staging Work?

Buyers are more responsive to staged homes in comparison to those that are not properly staged. If you fail to stage your home, you are only giving way for the competition to sell quicker than you and losing the opportunity to put more money in your pockets.

Staging has become a final touch for getting your home ready for the market. It also allows you to get the highest price for your home in the shortest amount of time.

Now that you understand the benefits of staging your home, let's check out a few hints to help you stage your home the right way:

Use Neutral Colors

This may cost you more cash and time, but it can help make a huge difference when it comes to getting your home off the market for the best price. Bright colors are great for people who want to show their personalities in their own home; however, for many buyers, it can be a serious turn-off.

The best things you can do for your home when staging it is to paint it using neutral colors like white and gray. Using loud colors can distract potential buyers from some crucial selling point of the home. Many buyers may love bright colors, but using neutral colors in the home will offer them the choice when it comes to doing so or not.

Clean and Clean Some More

This is common knowledge, but it is something lots of rehabbers miss. When you are placing your home on the market, the first thing to do is to clean it like never before. You want every part of the house to glisten.

A clean home tells a buyer that it is well taken care of. If there were certain areas you missed during the rehab, now is the time to make sure you clean all of it as best you can.

Keep Things Fresh

Placing too many extra items in the home can make it look cluttered. However, a few fresh, strategically placed flowers and plants can add some freshness and life to the house. Let them be properly spaced out, so they don't clutter a specific area, but ensure you place some fresh items in key areas.

Try to place some bright flowers or a little potted

plant in the living room or kitchen center table. If you are not a fan of fresh plants, you can use fake plants, as they perform the same role and last longer.

Another way of keeping things fresh is to ensure the home has no odor. A deep clean can help eradicate any smells left behind from the rehab, but you need to ensure there is no lingering odor that can welcome buyers during a showing. You could use some air fresheners or scented oils to make rooms smell more pleasant to buyers. Even so, remember not to overdo it as very strong smells, no matter how pleasant, can be a turn-off to most people, especially those with a sensitive sense of smell.

Let There Be Light

Dark rooms have a sad aura to them. Most buyers would prefer seeing bright rooms. This means lighting is a vital aspect of home staging. You can brighten up a room by allowing as much light as possible to shine in the home.

An easy way to do this is to open all the window blinds. In addition to bringing in more light, it will make the room look bigger to potential buyers. Make sure all the lights in the home are turned on during a showing, including lights in closets and lamps. It will ensure the house seems more welcoming and help the buyer figure out where to go next. Make sure you have appealing light fixtures, and if you have dingy or old-looking lampshades, try replacing them — toy around with numerous lighting types and temperatures to get the most alluring one.

First Stage the Vital Rooms

Staging the whole home is not a bad idea; nevertheless, if you don't have the time, begin by staging the essential parts of the house. The living room is the most important part when it comes to staging as this is the first place most buyers see when they head into a home. Next should be the master bedroom and then the kitchen. Additional bedrooms should be last on your list during a staging.

Rent Some Furniture

When renting furniture, you don't want to overdo it. A home with less furniture will look more appealing and larger to many buyers.

When the furniture comes in, position chairs, table, and couches from the wall, this is an approach known as "floating" the furniture. Ensure the space is anchored with an area rug as it helps in creating an intimate and comfortable space, great for having conversations with friends and family.

You want to ensure you have ample space to walk

around. It aids buyers in navigating the space and assists them in imagining their personal furniture in every room.

Don't Ignore the Curb

If the exterior of the property is not appealing enough, you probably won't get as many buyers as you should into the home. By making the curb appeal go up, you can draw more potential buyers into the home.

You can achieve this by following these tips:

- Wash the walkways and house

- Ensure your windows are clean

- Trim down overgrown shrubs and mow the lawns

- Plant beautiful flowers

- Make the house number is not difficult to read

- If there is a porch, add outdoor furniture

- Place potted plants and a welcome mat on your doorstep

Staging a home does not mean you have to spend a lot of cash. Instead, you need to make wise decisions. Once you have done everything in your power to show your home in the best manner possible, all that is left is to wait for the appropriate buyer to step in and get yourself ready for the closing process.

Chapter 15: The Closing Process

If this is your first time selling or buying a home, this can be a scary process. Not only do you need to get the timing right, but you also have a lot of work to do to ensure it is a successful transaction. If you are working alongside an agent, things may be a little easier, but you need to understand how to get the best of a deal as well.

Also, you need to understand how you can ensure you complete the sale promptly. So you don't waste your money and time during the process. We will be covering all of this in the next few pages. But first, let's see what closing means.

What Is a Closing?

Closing is the process whereby the house seller and buyer satisfy all of the promises made in the sales contract. It typically has to do with the transfer of documents and money so that you, as the seller, can transfer control and ownership of the property clear and free to the buyers. In addition to this, you will clear up all the remaining loans on the house and settle up with all the parties who helped in expediting the sale and closing.

Having covered this, let's take a look at what the closing process is like for you as a seller.

House Closing Process for Sellers

Negotiating

When a buyer makes you an offer, you are left with three choices:

- You can accept the terms if you find them suitable

- You can make a counteroffer and alter a few of the terms

- You can refuse the offer and walk away

You need to try to determine what inspires a buyer to purchase your property. If you know this, you will have the ability to negotiate terms aside from price. You can make them pay fees that would usually be yours to pay and ask them to cover specific repairs that may be found in an inspection. There are numerous ways you can get a great deal out of a sale without altering the price.

Don't let your emotions cloud your judgment during a negotiation. It is just business, and nothing is personal. You may still need something from a buyer before you close, and you don't want an angry buyer on your hands.

If you have many offers, you can play them off each other. Let all prospective buyers know that someone is offering higher and offer them the opportunity to alter their prices. Schedule a time and date for when you will accept the best offers. Anyone who has a serious interest in your property will provide feedback fast.

Take your time during negotiations but know that you have to create a balance, as you don't want it dragging on for too long. This aspect of the closing process should not take longer than three days. Going beyond this can make a buyer lose interest.

Closing Costs

For you as a seller, closing costs can add up for the buyer and yourself when you transfer the real estate title. You will need to pay title fees, closing fees, a part of the transfer taxes and all real estate taxes that have gathered and not been paid during the period of ownership.

Be ready to take responsibility for paying escrow fees, recording fees, lien releases, and repair fees, among others. Fees differ based on the state so you may be unable to provide a proper estimate for them but note that these costs can really add up. If you are working with a real estate agent, request that they provide an estimate of all the closing costs from the start. Note what the estimate consists of, so you can negotiate with prospective buyers as regards contingencies.

Agent Percentage

If you added a real estate agent to your team, based on your location in the US, you pay them 5 -7 percent of what you sold your property for. You will have to find out what the right rate is for your location. The seller typically pays the commission of the agent, and if there are a selling and buying agent, they both share the commission.

You can negotiate with agents with regard to their commissions, but it is not usually a great idea. Agents will focus on properties they get more money from, so if your property pays an agent less, the agent might focus on selling off other properties on their listing with promises of higher commissions. It is best to pay an agent what they are due to ensure you have their attention. Better still, you can offer a bonus for when they sell the property, as doing this can help you get a quicker sale.

Buyer's Due Diligence

Similar to your due diligence, your buyers will also

run due diligence on your property. The buyer's research is the same form of due diligence you run on a property before purchasing it, which we covered in Chapter 10. Its best to prepare yourself for any extra expenses you might incur.

Closing

As we covered earlier, closing is when the buyer offers cash to the seller in exchange for the deed of the property. The seller and the buyer have to be in the closing, with their attorneys (if needed), closing agent, and real estate agents.

If you are not going to be in attendance with your attorney, make sure you prepare your closing documents beforehand. If this is your first close, ensure you go through all the documents with your lawyer before closing, so you understand what you want to sign and agree to.

A disbursement sheet which outlines the amount of money the buyer has to bring to the closing table and the amount the seller leaves with will be put in place. Ensure the provisions are accurate, and they follow the conditions of the agreement of sale. You need to ensure that you are being offered the entitlement you deserve.

After all, the documents have been signed, and the

closing process is complete, ensure the amount of the cash you leave with tallies with what is owed to you on the disbursement sheet. If it fails to match, don't leave until it does. The disbursement sheet has to be accurate, as it is a legal record of the deal.

The property's title history will already have been revised by the title agency you are working with, and with any luck, they will have cleared any pending issues with the title. The title agent will be responsible for ensuring the figures align, gathering needed signatures, authenticating, and issuing checks. Keep a positive relationship with your closer, as they can make sure the process of closing is as smooth as possible or can make it a very hectic experience. The title company will also have the responsibility of putting the deed of the property on record with the local government.

For a seller, the closing process can consume a lot of time, especially if you are not prepared. Putting in as much as you need beforehand and being aware of what to anticipate will make the experience seamless for all parties involved.

When Is Your Property Categorized as Sold?

Your property could be categorized as sold at any point during the closing process. Still, in theory, your home has not been sold until you no longer have ownership. Your property is sold after the deed has been transferred and the money collected. Once that has happened, pat yourself on the back. You can now consider yourself a successful first-time house flipper.

Conclusion

Congratulations! You have reached the end of what could well prove to be a very lucrative journey. Rehabbing homes comes with a variety of possibilities, but also carries a lot of risks. Knowing these risks and preparing for them ahead of time is half to battle.

Don't forget to make a detailed plan before you go into this business or you may find yourself discouraged when you face problems down the road. Planning, communicating, and doing thorough research are all key when it comes to the process of flipping homes.

I have offered you all the essential information you need. All you have to do is to read, assimilate, and apply what you have learned efficiently, so the whole process is seamless for you, for your first flipped home and hopefully many more to come.

I hope you enjoyed this book as much as I enjoyed putting it together for you. Thank you and best wishes with all your real estate investment endeavors!